HOLLYWOOD

From Below the Line

A Prop Master's Perspective

Steven M. Levine

Robert D. Reed Publishers

Robert D. Reed Publishers • Bandon, Oregon

Robert D. Reed Publishers
P.O. Box 1992
Bandon, OR 97411
Phone: 541-347-9882; Fax: -9883
E-mail: 4bobreed@msn.com
Website: www.rdrpublishers.com

Editors: Deanna Hurst-Levine and Cleone L. Reed

Photographers for inside photos: Steven M. Levine and various prop assistants except for Pee-wee and bike photos, © Peter Sorel
Top cover photo: "Celebrity posing for paparazzi on red carpet" from fotosearch.com, pe0077568 © Tom Merton
Bottom cover photos: Steven M. Levine

Cover Designer: Deanna Hurst-Levine
Cover Graphic Artists: Periel Stanfield and Cleone L. Reed
Typesetter: Susan Leonard

ISBN: 978-1-934759-85-1
ISBN 10: 1-934759-85-6

Library of Congress Number: 2013955025

Manufactured, Typeset, and Printed in the United States of America

Dedication

To my soul mate and wife, Deanna.
Your encouragement convinced me that I could share
these stories to entertain and educate anyone who has an
interest in films or the filmmaking process.

To my children Derek and Danielle.
You have both enriched my life.

To my granddaughter Riley Grace "Bitty"
for keeping me very busy with all sorts of new and fun
things. BaBa loves you!

And to my Father, Allan,
who had enough faith in me to toss me into this line of
work to begin with. Without you, Dad, there would be no
book. May you rest in peace. We miss you.

Acknowledgements

To Bob and Cleone Reed of Robert Reed Publishers. Thank you for seeing this book's potential and for making the process for its release a fun and pleasant experience. I am sincerely grateful.

To Molly McKitterick for the original edit and the belief that the book was good enough to be published.

To Michael Badalucco for the awesome Foreword to this book. It's rare to find anyone who has walked on both sides of the line. Your work is amazing.

To my wife Deanna whose editing skills and obsession with punctuation, although annoying at times, made this a better book. Having you by my side in life and during the long process of writing this book has been a blessing, and I couldn't have done it without you.

To CDS Photo and Graphics in Hollywood for their assistance and support.

Table of Contents

Foreword

...Experiences of a Hollywood crew member:

The Daily Planet gleamed through the steamy night, a floodlit monolith rising like a beacon above the streets of Metropolis. Below was a gathering crowd craning with anticipation for a glimpse of the *Man of Steel*. Suddenly, without warning, all the surrounding streets went dark. The tall buildings were all black except for the few illuminated by the power of our generators. It was on 42nd street in the middle of Manhattan. I had a broom in my hand and was working as a set dresser. "Cut, Cut, Cut!" Not even the *Man of Steel* could save us. The great blackout of 1977 had begun.

I never did get to see *Superman* that night, but little did I know that 26 years later I would be acting along side Christopher Reeve on an episode of *The Practice*.

From 1976 through 1996, as a member of I.A.T.S.E Local 52, I worked in the prop department on movies, TV shows, and commercials. For most of that time I worked for Jim Mazzola, a legendary property master who is still at it. It was Jimmy, who in 1986 assigned me to work on the New York sequences for the film entitled *50*. That was when I met my first Hollywood property master, Steven Levine.

Experiences on movie sets have been well documented through the years, but what Steve offers us is something quite unique—a view from the trenches.

A property master's job is unlike any other on a film crew. He must know every detail of the script and have the ability to foresee the unforeseeable. He must be able to conjure things up on a moment's notice, must be a magician, a skilled mechanic, financial administrator, jack-of-all-trades, and a

Renaissance man. He must be able to construct a square box to fit into a round hole and make the shit hit the fan.

Where would Indiana Jones be without his bullwhip? Norman Bates without his butcher knife? James Bond without his vodka martini?

Hollywood From Below The Line brings to light the importance and integral nature of the property department to a film by bringing us inside the process. From the weeks of preparation before the cameras roll through the final wrap when the last director's chair is folded up, we gallivant through thirty-nine years of incidents and anecdotes. We also become privy to the effects of working 12 to 14 hours a day over the years, sometimes in distant locations, on one's family and personal life.

No stone is left unturned: from Robert DeNiro's method acting secrets, to Robert Mitchum's candid confession, we learn what it means to be "Pollacked" and what Leslie Nielsen was selling out of the trunk of his car. And that's just the tip of the iceberg.

Anyone interested in working in the movie business will find this to be informative, insightful, entertaining, and invaluable. Those of us who have been in the trenches should tip our hat to Steven, for this unabashed account of the daily grind.

Michael Badalucco
Emmy Award-winning Actor, *The Practice*

Preface

For as long as I have been working as a property master in the motion picture industry people have asked, "What is it like to work with movie stars?" or commented, "It must be so much fun to work in that business." The film industry has always had a mystique. Studio executives sitting in air-conditioned offices; producers, writers, and even the actors themselves have authored many books about this subject. This book is different. It is written by someone who is rarely, if ever, heard from: a crew member.

Known as "below the line" employees, our perspective is quite different from those you may have read in other books. On set twelve to fourteen and frequently sixteen hours a day, we are in the trenches. We have no motor homes to which we can retreat. We have no personal assistants running to Starbucks for us. We show up at call time and work straight through until wrap. Sometimes we are treated well and sometimes we are not. Often, we have to travel and be away from our families. The divorce rate is high. This is not a family-oriented business.

This book takes you on set with us. You will learn what working with the stars is like and experience life from behind the camera. You will get a better understanding of the amount of work that goes into the making of a motion picture or television program.

I hope as you read this book, you will be entertained as well as gain new insight into the on-set life of a crew member and, more specifically, how important props are to the look and feel and the authenticity of a production.

Enjoy,
Steven

CHAPTER 1

What Exactly Are Prop Masters and What Do They Do?

L et me begin by explaining what a prop is and the respons-ibilities of a property master on a film or television project. Simply, props are items actually handled or used in any way by the actors during the filming of a show (coffee mug, camera, gun, grocery bag, pen, football etc.). There are many additions to this that I will explain later in this chapter. The prop department is also responsible for the directors', producers', and actors' chairs. Don't get me started on this subject; it warrants a chapter of its own and is forthcoming.

The property master is the head of the prop department and hires an assistant or assistants according to the size of the project and the budget. For example, a film like *The Pirates of the Caribbean* is going to have several more assistants than a half-hour sit-com such as *Two and a Half Men*. A one-hour ep-isodic action series or drama for television like *24* or *Criminal Minds* will have between two and three full-time assistants, occasionally bringing in extra people or what are known as "day players" on particularly heavy days (days with big scenes that involve lots of background actors, known as "extras").

So now, let's take a simple example of the use of props. Visualize a scene with a lawyer entering a jail cell to converse with his new client. A jail keeper leads him to the cell and

1

opens it for him to enter. The lawyer enters, sits down, opens his briefcase, and pulls out a file that pertains to his client's case. The obvious and most likely scripted props would be the jailer's keys, the lawyer's briefcase, and the folder. But let's dig a little deeper into what the property master has to consider, beginning with the jail keeper.

He/she needs to be wearing a utility belt, which is a prop, not a piece of wardrobe. The first thing would be to find out the actor's waist size. Next would be to research what would be on an actual jail keeper's belt, which will vary depending on the city, county, or state in which the jail is located.

Would this person have mace, a baton, a radio, or maybe just keys and a walkie-talkie? Is the belt black or brown, smooth or basket weave? All principal characters will have what are known as "personal props" which include wedding rings, watches, pens, eyeglasses, and so on. These must all be shown to and approved by the director in advance.

Next, let's take the lawyer's briefcase. The property master will have shown briefcase choices to the director and will have the approved case plus a double (an exact match) if possible, as actors are notorious for leaving the set promptly with their props and then forgetting them in their dressing rooms. This makes it important to double principal props. Should there be a delay in shooting due to a prop left in a dressing room, it becomes the prop man's problem—not the actor's.

Now, for what's inside the briefcase. An attorney would have the case file. Keep in mind that no director wants to see a brand-new prop, as it would look straight out of the package, so careful attention must be paid to the aging of the folder. The inside of the folder also has to be accurate. It should be the same type of file that a lawyer would actually use, with the appropriate labels and markings. It must contain documents that refer to the case. If the camera happens to see into the file and it is filled with invoices from your last show, it will indicate to the director that you are not paying attention to detail. Plus, it gives the actor more to work with. It is imperative the case be properly outfitted with other files, legal papers, depositions, or anything else that a lawyer might carry.

If the lawyer wears glasses, they need to be pre-approved by the director and may need the actor's prescription lenses inserted. Next, they will need to have an anti-reflective coating applied so the director of photography doesn't see the lights reflected in the lenses.

Now, we should be ready to shoot—unless there are any last minute ideas from the actor or the director. Last minute requests are something we never like to hear. Any time we hear, "Wouldn't it be a good idea if...?" our blood pressure shoots through the roof.

There are several items that are not physically touched that still come under the prop master's jurisdiction. For example: vehicle license plates. More often than not, the scene takes place in a city or state that we are not really shooting in. Cars play an important role in most films so the license plate must reflect the appropriate state and period of time. If it is New York 1935, the plate needs to be accurately researched and then manufactured. There will need to be doubles for any principal vehicle, as frequently a "second unit" (an additional crew) will have a duplicate car and shoot at another location. So, duplicates are imperative.

The property master must put himself in each situation, as many props are not scripted. Here is a very simple example: If there is a doctor in the scene, it won't be scripted that he needs a stethoscope unless he specifically uses one to listen to a patient's heart. A prop man needs to know that a stethoscope is an obvious thing a doctor would have. We wouldn't be around long if we said to the director that we did not see a stethoscope written in the script. This illustrates the importance of picturing oneself at the location described and really giving thought to what would be of importance there.

Essential to keep in mind is that we are working within the confines of a budget that now more than ever is constantly being scrutinized. This means that should you have any ideas as to how you might be able to save money without sacrificing the director's vision, they need to be discussed with the producer and director, so that nothing is expected that you can't deliver. Sometimes even the biggest and most costly films have not been budgeted to anticipate or accommodate expensive last-minute requests. The un-realistic expectation of less-experienced producers is that the prop department should have everything needed at all times, yet still remain within the framework of the initial budget. Often, it's a struggle to find a happy medium. There have been times when I've had to jump through hoops just to get extra help for a very busy day (which amounts to a few hundred dollars), because there just isn't the money in the budget. However, when the writers come up with ideas and changes that can sometimes cost thousands of unbudgeted dollars, the money magically appears.

Food is the prop man's responsibility as well. If an actor needs to eat or drink, we must discuss with that person what she or he likes or doesn't like. Allergic to anything? Vegetarian? Frequently, actors will ask if their food can be fat-free so they do not ingest unnecessary calories. For big meals, party or restaurant scenes, I call in a "food stylist" so everything looks and tastes just right.

Small household pets, such as dogs, cats, birds, fish, etc., also fall under our jurisdiction. We might even have to get a horse or two, although the producers will handle the arrangements for a western or a scene that requires a larger number of animals. It can be a gray area, so communication is vital. Obviously producer input will be much more inclusive if we are casting an animal with a large or recurring role, like Lassie.

Over the years as the industry continues to evolve, the lines that were once very clear separating individual departmental responsibilities have become rather blurry, and things that really aren't prop issues are continually being thrown our way. In my opinion, this began when many talented young filmmakers graduating from film school were denied access to the unions. Frustrated at being excluded from union work, they were left with no choice but to forge ahead and produce their own non-union projects.

In film school, the young directors put their production designers in charge of the overall look of the show, relying on them to be certain that the props, set dressing, and wardrobe be true to the director's vision. When the unions finally opened their doors to these upcoming filmmakers, who by now had their own way of doing things, the gray areas that already existed between the prop master, the set decorator, and the art department in general began to grow larger. I found myself being asked to do things that had not been my responsibility in the past.

Anyway, I hope this gives you a basic understanding of a prop master's job and some of the challenges and dilemmas we frequently face. Much more will certainly be revealed in the stories that follow.

CHAPTER 2

Like Father, Like Son

Like Father...

I was born into the industry like many Hollywood employees. My father, Allan Levine, started in the laborer's union but rapidly moved into the property department. He climbed the ladder from set dresser to assistant prop master to property master in a very short period of time, just as I would do many years later. He worked on some of Hollywood's biggest budgeted and most popular films of his era. A partial list includes; the original *Dr. Doolittle, Tora Tora Tora, Three Days of The Condor, Jeremiah Johnson, Shampoo, All The President's Men,* and *Heaven Can Wait.*

As he worked on films, he began to collect valuable items he could eventually use as rentals, storing these items in several garages around the city; no public storage-type facilities were yet in existence. As a young boy, I tagged along, helping him arrange things to best make use of his limited space.

In 1973, he opened his first prop-rental house, The Hand Prop Room (HPR), on the old Desilu Studios lot in Culver City, California. By 1978, he moved it to its current location on Venice Boulevard in Los Angeles. He built it into the finest prop-rental facility in Hollywood attracting a large clientele.

It was, and still is, a "department store" for props where the thousands of items are neatly organized and displayed within a huge, two-story building, all divided into different categories, sections, aisles, and rooms. For example, if someone needs to rent an 1800's medical bag with appropriate instruments, medicine bottles, etc. or an authentic African tribal wedding-ceremonial item, The Hand Prop Room is the place to find them. My father traveled around the world purchasing items he knew would rent. He ventured into remote tribal areas in Africa to purchase exquisite indigenous items.

My father passed away in September of 1999. I am proud to say that he accomplished something quite amazing in his life. He forever changed the entire concept of prop-rental facilities, raising the bar and setting a new industry standard. Gone were the cluttered and dusty old prop warehouses with a randomly stocked inventory, and in came the highly stylized establishments that today serve as Hollywood's prop-rental facilities. At the time of his passing, HPR owned several items worthy of being displayed in museums. Independent Studio Services (I.S.S.) is another prop house that has blossomed into an amazing full-service facility, and History 4 Hire has done a terrific job specializing in vintage props as well.

* * *

Like Son...

As a small child I accompanied my dad to the studio to watch filming of *The Untouchables*, *The Greatest Show on Earth*, or *Kentucky Jones* while he was serving as property master. "The Untouchables" was particularly exciting because it frequently involved cars being blown up or Thompson machine guns being fired. The "Greatest Show on Earth" had wild animals on set that I also enjoyed.

Most of the people on the crew were friendly to me unless I accidently walked directly onto the set, which I quickly learned not to do.

As I got older my interest switched from gunfire and animals to the young starlets prancing around the lot. At that time, my father was working at 20th Century Fox Studios where a television series entitled *Land Of The Giants* was being filmed on Stage 17. The fact that I still remember the stage number of that show indicates how often I visited that particular stage in 1968!

However, it wasn't the show that drew me repeatedly to Stage 17. I was a big fan of the two girls with recurring roles named Deanna Lund and Heather Young. They wore very tight outfits and their breasts became objects of my fascination.

* * *

Shortly after graduating high school in 1970, I moved to downtown San Jose just a few blocks from the University. My group of high school friends attended school there, but I went to a local junior college instead.

If ever there was a time to live in Northern California that was it. Just south of San Francisco, the music scene was smokin'. Bands such as *The Grateful Dead, Santana, The Doobie Brothers* and *Jefferson Airplane* among many others were from that area. Blues music was predominant as well, and I attended several shows seeing some of the greats of all time. Studying was not high on my priority list, but I did become a scholar of pot smoking and beer drinking. In spite of the partying, I managed to get a two-year degree, but that was as far as my formal education went.

As the summer of 1973 began, I returned to live in Los Angeles with my father. Sadly, my mother had passed away four years earlier at the age of thirty-eight from a battle with breast cancer, so we were alone in the house. My plan was to spend a summer of fun and leisure and then return to San Jose for one more year of indulgence. For some reason, my dad had other plans.

He didn't approve of my beer drinking, pot smoking ways and without my consent, got me a job at CBS Studios in Studio City. The head of the prop department there agreed to give me a job for thirty consecutive days (weekends not included) that would qualify me to join the union. To remain in my father's house for the summer, I had no choice but to accept the assignment.

I was told to meet a fellow named George in the commissary at eight a.m. He would be looking for me as my dad told him to look for the young guy with long black hair. Wanting to make a good impression, I was there early. At eight o'clock sharp George approached me and asked if I was the prop man he was to hook up with. "No," I politely responded, "but my father is a prop man."

He then inquired, "Is your name Steven Levine?" When I answered in the affirmative, he informed me that I was indeed hired as a prop man and it would probably behoove me to be aware of that.

For the first week, I worked on the scoring stage where a full orchestra records music for specific scenes in film and television projects. My responsibilities were simple: setting up chairs and music stands for the musicians, etc. It was an easy job that I quite enjoyed. Incidentally, prop people no longer work the scoring stages and haven't for many years.

During the next five weeks, I worked as a set dresser. A set dresser is part of the set decorator's crew that puts the furniture, the paintings, and lamps, etc. onto the set. This was a substantially more difficult, time-consuming and detail-oriented job. Thankfully, at the conclusion of the six weeks I was laid off. I did join the union but immediately packed my car and headed north for one more year to enjoy being twenty-one years old.

When that year ended, I returned to Los Angeles, moved in with my girlfriend and began my life's experience of being a Hollywood film crew member.

CHAPTER 3

The Last Tycoon:
My First Major Motion Picture

Here I was, a twenty-three year old fledgling prop man working on a major motion picture. My father, Allan, was the property master; his main assistant was a fellow named David, who, like myself, was just starting out. I was low man on the totem pole.

Written in the script for *The Last Tycoon* was a very important personal letter to Monroe Stahr (Robert DeNiro) by his love interest in the film (Ingrid Boulting). The director was the very famous Elia Kazan who, among other major films, directed Marlon Brando in *On the Waterfront*. My father had very briefly introduced David and me to this legendary author and filmmaker at some point early in the preparation process of the film.

On this particular day, Allan decided that since David and I were going to be on set a good deal of the time, we should have the opportunity to meet Kazan again, this time in his office, to give him a choice of stationery on which the letter was to be written. Remember, directors always want to see things before they arrive on set, and they always want to see choices, particularly on "inserts" (props to be seen up close for the audience to get a good look at).

David and I, stationery choices in hand, nervously walk-ed up the old outdoor stairway at Paramount Studios in Hollywood and entered the corridor leading to Kazan's office. (Think of Dorothy and her friends approaching the great and powerful Wizard of Oz.) Once there, his secretary announced our arrival, the office door was opened, and we were ushered in to see *The Man*.

While trying desperately to exude confidence, we explained the reason for our visit, proudly displayed the stationery choices and anxiously awaited his decision. Kazan took a beat, looked up at both of us and bellowed, "Get the hell out of my office and never bother me with this type of shit again!" Without another word or a second's hesitation, David and I grabbed the stationery, ran back through the corridor, down the staircase, and headed directly to my father's office on Stage 5.

This incident is forever tattooed on my brain, as you may well imagine. My dad said very little and sent us on our way to continue our other assignments. At some point later that afternoon, while we were reviewing the day's accomplishments in our office, Kazan very casually came strolling in. David and I looked at each other like, *Oh God; we're getting fired before we even start shooting!* Instead, Kazan broke into a smile and apologized for what had happened and for scaring the living shit out of us.

The two amazing things about this were that not only did he apologize (not common among directors) but also he actually came to our office to do it. We never did find out if my dad asked him or if he had done this on his own, but just the fact that he did showed us he was a decent man and had some concern about his crew members. At any rate, we were far more careful in the future about when and where he was to be approached. By the show's conclusion, we had nothing but admiration and respect for this great film legend.

Recently, I was on the Paramount lot and walked past the same staircase thirty-five years after this incident occurred. It immediately brought back the memory and feeling as if it had just happened yesterday.

* * *

The Last Tycoon was filmed in 1976 before Robert DeNiro was a big star. There were plenty of other current stars of that era in the cast: Robert Mitchum, Tony Curtis, Ray Milland, Carl Malden, Donald Pleasance, Jack Nicholson, and Anjelica Huston, who at that time was Nicholson's on-again-off-again squeeze. Ingrid Boulting was a well-known model, and newcomer Theresa Russell went on to star in several other pictures but is probably most remembered for her role in *Black Widow*.

DeNiro's role as Monroe Stahr was patterned after the real-life Irving Thalberg, who had been a major player in the early days of big time Hollywood. There is a large office building on the Sony Studios lot named after him.

Being a method actor playing a large studio head, DeNiro would come in during pre-production, get into his wardrobe, come to our office, pick up his prop briefcase, watch, glasses, etc. and just walk around the Paramount lot as if he were truly the character he was about to play. This system obviously worked out very well for him.

One night, we were scheduled to film inside a guest-house located in the backyard of a Hancock Park mansion. Hancock Park is a gorgeous neighborhood located adjacent to Hollywood where wealthy, old-money families reside. In this particular scene, Monroe is very drunk and in the company of Theresa Russell's character. DeNiro started asking me for real cocktails earlier that day while we were shooting a large banquet scene at the old Biltmore Hotel in downtown

Los Angeles. I was getting used to doing just about anything actors asked of me; but for some reason, before I started getting him lubed up, I figured I had better ask my dad first. He explained to me that Kazan would have to be consulted because if we got an actor drunk without first checking with the director, we could be accused of holding up the company.

Kazan gave his blessing, and I started pouring. DeNiro drank for the rest of the afternoon, and asked for more when we arrived at "The Hudson House," the name of the Hancock Park location. By the time we were ready to shoot at around nine p.m., he was too drunk to do the scene.

Now everyone was scrambling; production assistants were bringing him coffee, ordering him food, and trying whatever other remedies they could think of. I just remember him lying with his head in Theresa Russell's lap and me being grateful that I had thought to check before serving up the cocktails that got him so drunk. As I recall, there was about a two-hour delay while he got sober enough to do the scene.

Most of us either hung out in the yard or retreated to our respective trucks to wait it out. Just to keep things lively while we were in the yard, Kazan suddenly clutched his chest and fell onto the grass as if having a heart attack. David and I were the first to get to him, yelling for help and trying not to panic. He popped up and blurted out, "Just kidding!" Looking back, I can laugh about it today, but at the time found it more scary than funny.

In those days while shooting on the Paramount lot, the stars had quarters similar to small ground-floor apartments that were used as dressing rooms or places to hang out between shots. When it was nearing time for an actor's scene and they were needed on set, either the second assistant director or a production assistant knocked on the dressing room door and let the actor know that they were being "invited" to set.

Mitchum, who had been a huge star and was now in the twilight of his career, had been busted for marijuana sometime in the '50s. Whenever he worked on this shoot, he came to the set fully prepared for his scene and rarely muffed his lines.

One of the assistant directors motioned for me to come with him to Mitchum's dressing room to invite him onto the stage for his scene. I had no idea why I was asked to go. I just followed along. We got there and knocked on the door. As soon as the door opened, we were immediately hit with a wall of marijuana smoke as Mitchum stepped out to join us. He didn't seem at all concerned that we had noticed the fragrant cloud. Nor did he appear to be under the influence. We accompanied him to the stage and watched while he effortlessly did his work.

The next time I saw him I told him it was hard to miss the smoke when we were at his room and asked if I might sample a bit myself. I had smoked my share of weed but had tapered off so I could be as sharp as possible in my new career. He happily obliged and later handed me a small bag.

I had all intentions of waiting for the end of the day to indulge, but the bag was burning a hole in my pocket as I was extremely anxious to see what type of weed a big-time movie star and devoted pot smoker had for his stash. I found an isolated spot and proceeded to take one moderately sized hit. *Wow, this tastes good!* I held it in, savoring it for a few seconds and exhaled a healthy dose of smoke. *Uh-oh—this shit is powerful.* I started to get a little paranoid but managed to hold it together.

A couple of minutes elapsed when I realized that I was far too stoned for a working environment, and I was having that mild but distinct feeling of, *Oh no, I'm starting to freak-out*. I began walking around trying to gather my thoughts and pull it together when I spotted Mitchum walking past. Fortunately he was by himself. I walked up to him and mentioned that I had just sampled his stuff, which I found to be quite strong.

This was his response: "It's the Devil's weed son; I grow it myself." That didn't make me feel any better but I thanked him just the same for the information and continued on my walk, praying I wouldn't be seen or have to engage in any conversation. I don't recall ever smoking the rest of what he gave me, but if I did, I damn sure didn't do it at work!

CHAPTER 4

10

In 1978 I received a call from a property master who asked me to be his assistant on *10*, the Bo Derek/Dudley Moore film directed by Blake Edwards, famous for all of those *Pink Panther* movies starring Peter Sellers. Bo was a newcomer and married to the much older John Derek who had previously been married to Linda Evans and Ursula Andress, two famous beauties of their era. The guy sure had an eye for the babes! He left Linda Evans for Bo when she was just eighteen years old. Dudley went on to do a string of movie hits that included *Arthur* in which he played the inebriated but lovable title character.

It is hard to believe but at the time of this writing, it has been thirty-five years since our preparation for *10* began. I would like to share with you the incidents that really stand out in my mind.

To begin with, Dudley was an excellent pianist and there were pianos on several of the sets. He would sit down and just play these incredible songs ranging from jazz to classical, from boogie-woogie to blues. There seemed to be no genre he couldn't play. I remember shooting in a church with a huge pipe organ, and Dudley played it with the same skill he demonstrated on the piano. He was also a very cordial fellow, and I respected him for his various talents.

A prominent scene in the film takes place in a lovely backyard situated in the mountains, with a beautiful view of the ocean in the distance. In this scene, Dudley's character, under the influence of pain medication and alcohol due to an unpleasant dental appointment, is looking through his outdoor telescope when he spots a party going on in the backyard below. All the attendees are completely naked. He proceeds to lose his balance and roll down the huge hill, winding up in the yard full of the naked people.

In real life, these were pornographic movie actors, and to say that they were uninhibited would be quite an understatement. There's one scene where Dudley is in the middle of two girls with his arms wrapped around them. The beginning of the shot starts with the audience only seeing the three of them from the waist up. As they walk forward and the camera pans around behind them, the audience sees their naked backsides. It's assumed, of course, that their fronts are naked as well. That is in fact a safe assumption because to obtain this shot, Dudley did indeed have to be completely nude in front of the entire crew. When the cameras were ready to roll, he would drop his underwear and commence with the scene.

I have to say, he was truly a good sport about it, and by now, the crew had come to know him well so everyone was laughing, including Dudley. I vividly remember watching him giggle, but when Blake yelled "Action!" he snapped right into character, a testament to the true professional that he was.

As I said, the porn actors, including a very prominent female performer of the time, were the most uninhibited folks I have ever seen. They were perfectly comfortable just hanging around the backyard in their birthday suits while the crew prepared for the upcoming shot. They had all been given robes to wear, but what the hell, it was hot, so most didn't bother to put them on.

A particularly buxom girl from the group was sitting in the yard reading the newspaper. As she was sitting enjoying the sun and the news, grips walked by with their equipment, electricians cruised by with lights and gels—various crew members getting their normal work done as quickly and efficiently as possible. What made this so surreal was the girl reading the paper was totally naked, with one leg propped up on a lounge chair. She appeared not to be phased in the least sitting there undressed, any more than she would be if she were fully clothed and in her own living room. I'm surprised there weren't some accidents.

Another funny sight was seeing them all lying around the yard catching some rays between takes. I heard one of the male stars being called to set. He had been lazily lounging in the buff when he hopped off his chair and jogged toward the camera with his foot-long member flopping up and down, sideways and every which way until he arrived at the designated spot. I could have lived without that visual! However, a highlight for me that day was seeing the still photographer snapping pictures of two girls in action. It was a little difficult getting back into work mode after that.

The most outstanding event happened at the end of the last day that we were using the porn actors. Blake decided that we needed a still photo of them in all their glory as a remembrance of their appearance in the film. I seem to recall that there were about forty of them. As they positioned themselves, about half of them had their robes on and half did not. Just before the photo was about to be taken, it was requested that those wearing robes remove and drop them.

Now placed and ready for the memorable snapshot, Blake asked that the robes at their feet be taken away so as not to be seen in the photo. As a rule, the prop person checks and gets rid of any unwanted items left in a shot. Instinctively I ran in to remove the robes from the ground as quickly as possible.

Just imagine my view as I diligently made my way between the rows of naked men and women, scooping up the robes as I was running in a crouched position, at about mid-body height so I wouldn't have to keep bending over and standing back up for each one, while at the same time trying to avoid bumping into any of them.

One of my favorite days on set was filming the scene when Dudley finally woos Bo into his hotel room and into bed. Bo's action was to get out of bed to put on *Bolero*, a famous classical piece she wanted to hear while making love. After each take, it was my job to re-set the record and cover her back up in bed. Bo had been offered a robe, but found putting it on and taking it off between takes to be too much of a hassle, so she eliminated it. *Fine with me.*

At the completion of principal photography I went with a second unit to Hawaii for additional shots. It was an easy and enjoyable assignment for me, and I got to stay at a luxurious hotel on the north shore of Oahu for a week.

It was less than one year from wrapping *10* when I received my first opportunity to be the property master on a "little movie" entitled, *Airplane.*

CHAPTER 5

Airplane

The year was 1979 and I had a moderate amount of assisting under my belt. This "little movie" that would later turn out to be a huge financial blockbuster was about to go into pre-production.

Airplane was a low-budget film to which Howard Koch, a major Hollywood producer, and Paramount Studios had given the green light. It was to be directed by three unknown talents who had founded the Kentucky Fried Theatre, a small but successful theater company in Los Angeles. These were two brothers originally from Shorewood, Wisconsin (Jerry and David Zucker) and Jim Abrahams, their long-time friend. This was the beginning of a long and prosperous career for all three of them as *Airplane* would go on to be one of the largest grossing comedies of all time.

My father worked with Mr. Koch on the *Untouchables* starring Robert Stack, who was also to appear in the film. He had heard about *Airplane* and gave Mr. Koch a call, which culminated in my landing the property master position and also successfully launched my career at the age of twenty-seven. Actually, I was apprehensive about accepting this assignment as I really did not feel ready to head my own department, but with my father's coaxing and his assurance to oversee my work, I went ahead with it.

The script was full of props and gags and was quite a challenge. Somehow I was able to succeed even with the limited amount of experience I had at that time. To this day I remain very proud of my achievement on this film. When you watch it with more "prop" awareness, I think you'll get a sense of what an accomplishment it was for a first-time property master.

In retrospect, having the amount of experience that I now have, I might have done some things differently, mostly having to do with the administrative aspect of the job, like budgeting. But when it came to the set, we were on top of it. Everything that was required from my department was there without fail, and we never once held up the camera with prop delays.

Having only one assistant, I had to not only work the set daily, but had to simultaneously keep up with organizing and making sure all of the props needed in the days to come were ready. I did have about six weeks of pre-production (six weeks may sound like a lot of time, but trust me, it's not excessive) during which I did the bulk of preparation and acquisition of props, but there were still phone calls and things that needed daily attention during the course of the shoot (not to mention the last-minute ideas that would come up either during a rehearsal or sometimes right before the cameras were about to roll).

One funny memory is that of a scene at the airport depicting the Peter Graves' character, *Captain Oveur*, checking out magazines at an airport bookstand. The magazines are separated into categories labeled Fiction, Nonfiction, and Whacking Material. *Captain Oveur* is looking at a magazine which I had manufactured entitled, *Modern Sperm*. For the bulk of the "Whacking Material" I had gone to a local XXX-rated establishment to purchase enough girly/porn magazines to fill the needed space on the rack. I carried my large stack of "whack mags" up to the counter. Now before I continue, you need to understand that for me to be reimbursed for purchased items, I'm required to turn in the corresponding receipts. Okay, that being said....

The clerk rang up the sale, which I'm sure was substantially larger than his usual transactions. Nonetheless, he nonchalantly took my money, bagged the items, gave me my change, and thanked me. He did not, however, offer me a cash register receipt so I had to ask for one. The expression on his face told me that my request had caught him off guard and also apparently annoyed him as he sarcastically asked, "What are you going to do, deduct these from your income taxes?"

As the first day of shooting approached, my anxiety level rose. I will never forget the way I felt the night before that first day and how I felt in the morning on the drive to work, knowing that *this was it*... the cameras were about to roll. I had never been so nervous in my entire life.

The first scene filmed on the first day actually appears near the end of the film. It was to be shot in the cockpit with *Striker* (Robert Hayes) and the stewardess (Julie Hagerty) trying to land the plane. The gag is that *Striker* starts sweating profusely, becoming soaking wet. Our special effects crew hooked up small tubing to a Hudson Sprayer and hid the tubing in Robert's hair. Once that was accomplished and the cameras rolled, the effects guys started pumping the Hudson Sprayer and water began pouring through the tubes creating the excessive sweating effect.

The prop department supplies towels to dry the actors or clean up spills, that sort of thing. I already had plenty of towels prepared for this, but due to my extreme nervousness, I had gotten about five miles from home that morning, started to panic, and decided I had better go back and get more towels, which of course was unnecessary. I've since come to realize that the first day of shooting feels like the first day of school times ten.

Of course, everybody's in the same boat; and on the first day, no one feels very comfortable as everyone is busy and just praying that if something goes wrong it doesn't have anything to do with them or their department. As I recall, the first day went fine for my assistant and me; I felt as if we were off to a decent start. Whew!

If you have seen the movie, you'll recall that an on-board crisis begins when the pilots and passengers become ill from eating fish. The co-pilot (Kareem Abdul-Jabaar) and the first mate are asked what they had for dinner to which they both reply, "The fish." The Captain (Peter Graves) is then asked what he had for dinner. To emphasize the point that he also had the fish, we shot an insert of his completed dinner plate with the obvious skeleton of a fish plucked clean. With my limited amount of experience at that time, I was trying my very best to get all of the props exactly as they wanted, naively paying less attention to my budget than I would from that point forward in my career.

In retrospect, I probably could have gone to the fish market, cooked up a large fish, and scraped it clean, leaving only the bones. Instead, I had the Hand Prop Room research department find a perfect fish skeleton from a museum gift shop that was perfect for the shot. HOWEVER, the cost of the skeleton was more than my bosses were expecting to pay. The line producers (producers in charge of the money) immediately let me know they were less than thrilled. But realizing I was new and this was my first show, they explained to me, making it very clear, that the prop budget was my responsibility and just as vitally important to monitor as the props that I put in front of the camera. Embarrassing... but... lesson learned, moving forward...

Except that the first assistant director (let's call him Arnie)—whose business it was absolutely none of—found out about the inflated price of the fish skeleton. Arnie was the type of person who was so desperate to climb the ladder he would do anything, at anyone's expense, to appear as the hero. Apparently doing only his job would not suffice. No, he needed to stick his nose in everyone else's business as well, searching for anything remotely resembling something that he could make an issue out of and then fix it. So, it's no surprise he took great pleasure in letting everybody, including our three directors, know just how much the fish cost the company.

I approached him about the fact that the mistake had already been addressed and resolved and that he should mind his own business. He never did. I didn't it know it then, but I would be faced with this type of individual throughout the course of my career.

There was much I needed to learn about the politics of this business as well as honing the skills and ingenuity required to do this job. When all was said and done *Airplane* was an enormous success and to this day is known as one of the all-time great comedies. Not a bad credit to kick off my career.

* * *

One of the first props to be discussed in the production meeting was Otto, the co-pilot. Otto was an inflatable, blow-up doll that was a major part of our cockpit crew. The truth, however, was that Otto had air constantly being pumped through him with a fan to keep him upright.

The executive producer, Howard Koch, told me where I could have Otto manufactured. It was the same company that had made giant inflatable versions of the Oscar statue, which were used at an actual Academy Awards Ceremony. It turned out they were willing to make Otto, a backup Otto, and a female counterpart for Otto to be used in the film's final sequence. They also made an inflatable life vest shaped like a duck that the second stewardess (Lorna Patterson) used to demonstrate to the passengers the proper way to use a life vest.

Remember the model plane given to little Joey in the cockpit by Peter Graves during the famous scene when he asks the little boy if he liked gladiator films or had ever seen a grown man naked? I bought that plane on a location scout at the LAX airport. (I sure wish I still had that thing... talk about a great piece of movie memorabilia.)

Very early in the filming, we all noticed that whenever Leslie Nielsen was on set, he seemed to have a serious case of gas. He appeared to fart in front of the crew with no embarrassment whatsoever. He would let one fly and then say something like, "Oops, sorry; I must have had too much melon this morning" or, "Pardon me, something must not have agreed with me." He had lots of excuses. We were all a little suspicious, figuring no one could be that gassy, and in fact our suspicions were confirmed; he wasn't.

He had a small gadget that he concealed in his hand that was made of two bottle tops with a hollow rubber tube connecting them. One of the tops had a hole in it and when properly placed and squeezed would emit the best, simulated fart you have ever heard. I even saw him use it on a late-night talk show. There was simply no limit to his enjoyment of the little thing. He sold me one from the trunk of his car for seven bucks. I became quite adept with it myself, never quite acquiring Leslie's skills, however.

Once there was a woman visiting the set observing the day's work, sitting in a director's chair. I happened to notice

Leslie casually strolling up next to her. He stood there quietly for a moment and then gave his favorite little toy a squeeze. Out came the perfect fart. She turned and looked at him with shock. Leslie didn't flinch or react at all. Keeping his gaze straight in front of him, he acted as if nothing had happened. A few seconds passed, and he ripped another one. This time she looked at him with disgust and said, "You know, you are really very rude."

He apologized and gave her one of his many lame excuses for having uncontrollable gas, then sheepishly walked away never letting her in on his secret. She turned, shook her head and looked at me like *can you believe that guy*? I could barely contain my laughter.

I was a bit star-struck with Kareem Abdul-Jabaar, who at the time was in the midst of his unparalleled career. One day there was a break between the scene Kareem had just finished and the scene he was to be in later that day. I saw him go up to Arnie and ask him if he had time to go to his gym located nearby before he was needed again. Arnie, like many assistant directors would do, told him no, he didn't think that would be a good idea. Kareem then proceeded directly to his car and left for the gym. When he returned there was plenty of time to spare. I must say I really enjoyed witnessing Kareem blowing off Arnie like that!

Howard Koch was on set the entire time, from day one through wrap, something I have rarely seen an executive producer do since. He was a brilliant old-school producer and he knew every aspect of filmmaking. He made damn sure the directors stayed on schedule. Several times, I heard him yell out, "Okay, you have one more take and we are moving on!" The directors listened and did just what he said.

All of us in this business have been on shows that routinely shoot fourteen to sixteen hours daily with the director having all power and no one to reel him/her in. Take after take, angle after angle, be it television or feature film, some days seem to go on forever. The funny thing is, with all the extra money that it costs the company in overtime hours, and the amount of unnecessary footage shot, it doesn't guarantee a better film or television show.

One well-known and highly respected filmmaker, let's call him Clint Eastwood, shoots only an average of ten-hour days. He knows what he wants, comes prepared, and when he sees the performance he likes he prints it and moves on. I heard he made *Million Dollar Baby* in about thirty-seven days and brought it in ahead of schedule and under budget. According to my credible sources, very few of the days were extremely long. As you know, it won Best Picture of the Year.

Eastwood is also one of the most loyal people in the business, using basically the same crew film after film. Those lucky enough to work with him have nothing but praise for him. His body of work is incredible, and in addition to his outstanding work as an actor (excluding his performance to an empty chair), he has become one of Hollywood's most successful and beloved directors. I always hoped for the chance to work with him and would to this day welcome the opportunity, but he used the same property master for many years. When that fellow retired, Clint—true to his reputation for loyalty—promoted his assistant.

On *Airplane* Howard did much of the same, keeping us on budget and on schedule with reasonable hours.

One of my funniest memories was the scene with the "shit hitting the fan." In this case, the shit was a prop so I had to come up with something that would resemble poop. I went to the store and bought a copious amount of that re-fried bean potato chip dip, some canned corn, some caramel coloring and an assortment of other ingredients. John, our special-effects coordinator, and I mixed up a huge batch made from my ingredients and added a few items from the craft service table for good measure. If I remember correctly, even Howard Koch and some other interested parties joined in the shit-manufacturing festivities. The end result looked pretty good... well, as good as shit can possibly look.

When it came time for it to hit the fan, John loaded the faux poop in an air gun. I turned on the fan when they yelled, "Roll!" On action, John pulled the trigger. Strike! Mission accomplished. It looked amazing and if you watch closely, you can even see a nice chunk plop off of the blade and onto the table.

There was also a scene that required a watermelon to splatter on the control room floor to demonstrate the consequences if *Striker* were unable to properly guide the plane down onto the runway without the landing gear working. I bought a host of melons, climbed up to the catwalks high above the stage floor and took aim at the general vicinity where they wanted the watermelon to land. The cameras rolled, the line of dialogue that was my cue for action was delivered and BOOM, I dropped the melon about forty feet straight down. SPLAT! Bingo, a perfect hit.

Toward the very end of shooting, we shot the opening sequence of the film at LAX where the huge nose of a plane crashes through a giant plate glass window. The nose of the plane was built and mounted onto the back of a large flatbed truck, facing the opposite direction of the truck's front. So on action, the driver put the truck in reverse and backed that nose right through the floor-to-ceiling, wall-to-wall window. It was the most unbelievably awesome sight to watch in person. The sound of the crashing glass was astounding. That's one of those scenes where everyone on set is holding their breath because even though they have several cameras filming from different angles at the same time, they only get one chance, one take, so it better be perfect.

A little movie trivia: That scene was set up by a tarmac worker becoming distracted by another worker who misdirected the plane which in turn caused the "mishap". The worker with the flashlights in the scene is Jerry Zucker, and the guy who distracts him is David Zucker.

CHAPTER 6

Hard Country

Just after completing *Airplane,* I was hired to do a feature film entitled *Hard Country. Hard Country* was trying to ride the heels of the success of the John Travolta/Debra Winger hit, *Urban Cowboy.* It failed to hit the mark by a long shot. What it did do was launch the very successful film career of Kim Basinger, this being her first feature film. I have not worked with or seen her in person since, but she was a very pleasant and lovely person to work with. The cast also included Jan-Michael Vincent and Michael Parks of *Then Came Bronson* fame, a '60s TV series about a guy cruising around the country on a Harley-Davidson Sportster. A very young Daryl Hannah was featured, playing the younger sister of Jodie (Kim Basinger's character). In addition, there was a special appearance by country music's legendary Tanya Tucker. I particularly loved seeing her perform, as I've always been more "star struck" by great athletes and musicians than actors.

Hard Country, although set in Texas, was shot in Bakersfield, California (doubling for Texas), and on stages and local locations in Los Angeles. It was 1980 and I had a "Disco Sucks" bumper sticker on my pickup truck and wore a cowboy hat, for reasons I cannot recall. David Greene, our director, was quite eccentric. A veteran television director in his mid sixties, he had wild gray hair, a goatee, and a rather short fuse. Still, we got along very well. My assistant and I were the first recipients of his parting gift to the crew, a paperweight with his name and the year and title of the film etched into it. He was married at the time to Vanessa, a much younger English girl, whom he split with during filming and took up with an even younger wardrobe girl.

Once, about fifteen of us crew members were with him in a minivan, scouting locations. David was riding in the front passenger seat. He turned to us and asked, "Anyone mind if I have a smoke?" Being crew members, none of us were going to say no, and it wasn't that unusual a question back then. I remember him pulling out a silver cigarette case. But instead of pulling out a cigarette, he whipped out and fired up a doobie right there in the van and proceeded to smoke it all by himself! He never mentioned a word about it, or offered to share. He just smoked as much as he wanted, put it out, and set it back in its case. We all looked at each other in amazement, but of course no one said anything, and our day continued as if nothing had occurred.

David, being English, expressed himself in that distinctly British way. You know... that certain phrasing and use of words along with the accent that makes just about anything sound sophisticated and proper. Well, he sprang an interesting expression on me one day while we were shooting exteriors in Bakersfield. I was standing next to him as another crew member that shall remain nameless walked by with a large dog in tow. Out of the blue David turned to me and said, referring to the guy, "Steve, I don't like that man; he's a cunt!" *Okay then.* I soon came to understand that apparently that word is used differently and fairly often by some Brits.

* * *

For our filming on *Hard Country*, what had been an empty building in Bakersfield was transformed into the local watering hole, "The Stallion." The scenes to be shot needed a large group of extras, but the production company didn't have the budget for as many as were needed. They came up with the brilliant idea of advertising for extras to work for all the free beer they could drink. *This is going to be interesting.* I had already contacted beer companies in Texas, offering them exposure in the film for free cases of beer. As I recall, the beers used were Lone Star, Pearl, and Shiner. The companies came through with an adequate supply of brew, getting plenty of exposure. I was provided with an old refrigerated milk truck to keep the stuff cold, which it did not do, but no one seemed to mind, particularly after the fifth beer.

Filming tends to take a long time and can get pretty boring, and beer tends to get you drunk, which evidently escaped or never entered the minds of the brainy execs. This combination created quite a fluctuation in the amount of extras we had available throughout the day. So the assistant director tried to stage the shots with the most extras needed within the first half of the day, as drinking heavily and then being ordered to be quiet doesn't always work. I have to say that I don't recall any fist fighting, for which I was both surprised and thankful.

There was one scene where Kyle (Jan-Michael) has a beer-chugging contest with another character. The beer pitchers I used were quite large as per the director's instruction. The guy competing with Jan-Michael in the scene requested non-alcoholic beer. Having been around Jan-Michael, I was not surprised when he requested room temperature Heineken. Back then he was known to be a bit of a wild man. I went to our director and told him of Jan's request, which he granted. He knew Jan would be drunk;

but he also knew that if he said no, he wouldn't get his scene. I loaded both pitchers with their respective beers; the actors were in place and the cameras rolled. You can see for yourself—should you be able to find a copy of this film somewhere—that Jan did it all in one take with no cuts. I was impressed.

* * *

Back in Los Angeles on the last night of shooting, I was standing outside the stage when David walked up to me. Kim had just walked off of the stage and headed toward her trailer. He looked at me, then back at Kim and said, "She has it all, Kim does; she will be a very big star soon." He was certainly right about that.

David passed away in 2003 at the age of eighty-two. To my knowledge, *Hard Country* was the only feature film he ever directed, but he was one of the most sought-after television directors for many years. He directed classics including *Rich Man Poor Man* and *Roots*.

CHAPTER 7

The Prop Master's Script Breakdown

The prop breakdown is a critical first step in getting our end of the show together. What I do when I receive a script is read it cover to cover and get the gist of the story. When finished, I will read it again, but this time, I will make notes on the script pages of any important ideas or details I come up with that are not written in the script.

For example, the script direction reads: "Adam pulls up to the station and exits his police car." I will make a note to research a police car and its decals from whatever city we are supposedly in. We will then have those graphics replicated to match an actual police car as closely as possible, frequently making small adjustments for clearance issues. If it is a fictitious city, the production designer will come up with what he and the director like, and we will have everything custom made. Many cop cars have specific bumper stickers and roof top numbers that need to be created, and the license plates must also be made. The graphics company I use has both past and present research on plates. They then fabricate plastic replications on a vac-u-form machine.

Maybe the scene calls for a mom or dad dropping off a child in front of a middle school. I will note all the necessities needed like backpacks, lunch boxes, binders, schoolbooks, skateboards, bicycles, etc.

Now it is time to start the actual breakdown. The breakdown consists of all of the props needed for the entire show separated into different categories such as rentals, purchases, manufacturing, weapons, graphics, food, etc. This breakdown will not only specify the required props, but once completed, will be the foundation for the budget. The budget tends to be tricky because it is necessary to include extra money for props that will come up during a rehearsal or from a director's last-minute brainstorm. It isn't wise to tell the director that there is no room in the budget for his idea, particularly if it is relatively inexpensive. The more expensive props need to be exactly as discussed with the producer or director, as no one has the budget to supply choices or last-minute requests on expensive items without first getting approval.

The production manager will have a figure pertaining to our budget that "The Suits" want met, but the person who generates that figure usually only budgets money for what is scripted, leaving little room for creativity. I generally figure my budget on the high end and then add 10% for unforeseen situations.

This is where the game begins. Production managers normally won't volunteer their figure. They want to hear our estimate first. Should we be under their figure, they will tell us not to go over the amount we just quoted. Most likely, however, our quote will be higher than theirs, at which time they will inform us, "Your figure is too high and will need to be discussed further to see what can be brought down or eliminated." Directors almost never want to eliminate. Production managers generally don't like to add.

We may or may not go back and forth depending on the discrepancy in the amounts, but one thing is for damn sure; if you try to save money by matching or coming in below their quote at the expense of not giving the director what he/she wants, you will surely be fired. Trust me; no one will go to bat for you explaining that you were just trying to be frugal. You will simply be replaced.

On the other hand, you cannot go to the extent of completely overspending either, giving the director choices on too many items or trying to anticipate their every whim. During the course of prep, you must have conversations with the director and other departments that may intersect with what you are planning to do, and come up with the best way possible to not only appease the director, but to make the bean counters happy too. As long as the director is happy with what you are providing, it is rare that you would be dismissed, even if you should happen to go over budget.

Let's examine how to do a prop breakdown. In a script, each scene is numbered and identifies the location of the scene. Then the action and dialogue are added. In the following little story that I concocted, I have put props or anything pertaining to props in bold type to illustrate this process:

Sc.1–Ext. Office Building–Morning

William (discuss personal props with director i.e. eyeglasses, wristwatch, etc.), early thirties, handsome and single is entering the foyer of a large office building where he is a life-insurance salesman for a large and prominent firm.

As he enters, **briefcase** in hand, he spots a beautiful **young woman (she may have a prop in hand, i.e. coffee or briefcase, etc.)** exiting the building through the large glass doors. He cranes his neck to get a good long look when he walks directly into Frank, a co-worker, **cup of coffee** in hand and dressed for the day's work. The coffee spills all over Frank's sports jacket.

William

"Jesus Christ, Frank I am so sorry." William pulls out his **handkerchief** and begins to wipe the coffee off of Frank's jacket. "Let me take your jacket to my cleaners and he'll make it good as new; I promise."

Frank, mid forties, is a no-nonsense type wearing **thick glasses that are ten years out of date**. He is about forty pounds overweight.

Frank

"What the hell were you looking at anyway, William? Most people walk with their head facing the direction they are going."

Shaking his head, Frank turns to walk to the bank of elevators leading up to his office. As the elevator door opens and Frank enters, **two men** quickly follow him in, pulling **ski masks** down over their heads. The doors close, and Frank is trapped inside the elevator with the **masked men**, who now pull the stop button on the elevator and stick a **gun** in Frank's fat belly. **(Weapons and masks to be discussed with director.)**

Sc. 2—Interior – Elevator

The action and dialogue continue to be described for each scene until the conclusion of the story. This gives you a quick idea of how a script is laid out. Now we list all of the categories that the props would be listed under:

- Prop Purchases
- Props Manufactured
- Prop Rentals
- Props Printed and Graphics
- Weapons/Rubber Doubles
- Prop Food
- Promotional props
- Animals
- Expendables (supplies)
- Miscellaneous

Let's now take our one scene from above and separate our props into the appropriate categories:

1. William's briefcase   Purchase

2. Wristwatch for William   Purchase

3. Briefcases for background/extras   Rental

4. Coffee cups and drink holders   Purchase

5. Handkerchiefs   Purchase

6. Paper towels to wipe up
   coffee for take two   Expendables/Supplies

7. Eyeglasses for Frank   Manufacture
   (add his correction if needed and anti-reflective coating)

8. Cell phones for background/extras   Rental

9. Newspapers for background/extras   Purchase

10. Masks for bad guys   Manufacture

11. Guns for bad guys	Weapons
12. Rubber weapons to match	Rental

**Note—if later in the script gunfire takes place, it would be necessary to add full, half, or quarter-load blanks to the breakdown.

The guns we use are real weapons plugged to fire blanks. If not being fired, realistic looking replicas can do the trick. Should the gun be dropped, kicked, or used to hit someone, rubber weapons become necessary.

In addition, property masters have prop boxes (drawers and shelved lock boxes used to store props that we have purchased or acquired over the years) that we keep on the prop truck. We carry a supply of jewelry, sporting goods, toiletries, medical equipment, small electronics, men's and women's wallets, key chains, kitchen supplies, etc., that often come in handy. This is just an auxiliary source from which to draw (mostly for emergency/last-minute requests); it doesn't include the specific props needed for the particular show we are working on at the time.

Most of us own prop trailers anywhere from thirty to forty-eight feet long where we keep our boxes and basic equipment. The most unique prop truck I've ever seen is actually a renovated old school bus equipped with a futon (should there ever be an opportunity for a quick rest). It's owned by Leonard, who lives in New Orleans and was my assistant on *True Blood* for the portion we shot in Baton Rouge. Louisiana is far from a comfy location in the middle of the summer: swamps, mosquitoes, 100-plus degrees with ninety-eight percent humidity and mostly outdoor locations including one that required us to film a full day on a blacktop two-lane highway. To survive that day I had to strap an ice bag onto my head.

CHAPTER 8

Cocoon

One of the best things that came out of working on *Hard Country* was getting to work with the first assistant director, Jan Lloyd, who was also the assistant director for Ron Howard on the films, *Night Shift* and *Splash*. A couple of years later, I was on the 20th Century Fox lot and bumped into Jan and he told me he was about to go into pre-production on a film for Ron. I asked if they had a property master signed for the project, and as luck would have it, they didn't. He offered to set up a time for me to meet with Ron to interview for the position.

I knew I would be up against other prop masters, but I felt that I would be a good fit for Ron. I was excited about the prospect of working with the young upcoming director, who not only had supreme directorial talents, as we had seen in his two previous films, but also someone who I had watched grow up on television as *Opie Taylor* and *Richie Cunningham*. My interview went well, and I got the job.

There was one problem that needed to be addressed, however. I had been offered a television series called *Paper Dolls* a short time prior to meeting with Ron. My start date with *Dolls* was still a month away, so although I knew it might be slightly frowned upon to back out, I also knew that I was giving production more than enough time to replace me with any number of well-qualified prop masters looking for work.

So I called the producer of the series, let's call her Joan, and explained the situation. By her reaction, you would have thought the star of the show had backed out. I must say, I was pretty shocked by her emphatic promise that not only would I never work for *her* in the future, but she would make sure that I would never work for *anyone* she knew either! *Wow, what an egomaniac.*

As upset as I was, I wasn't about to dwell on it as I had a big job ahead of me that I was very much looking forward to. That choice worked out in my favor because *Paper Dolls* lasted only one season and I went on to do three feature films for Ron.

My son, Derek was three years old at the time and my daughter Danielle was just turning two. The film was all to be shot in St. Petersburg, Florida, and since the kids were so young, my first wife Vicki was able to bring them with her for the entire time. We found a nice apartment on a beautiful golf course. I left Los Angeles about three weeks prior to their arrival to attend meetings and rehearsals. It also made sense to acquire some of the props there as opposed to bringing them from L.A. My assistant, Mark, stayed back in Los Angeles to continue with the prep work and get the prop truck ready to travel to location.

I was somewhat nervous for the flight to Florida so I took a ten-milligram Valium as we were leaving the gate. I was in a middle seat between two older businessmen dressed in suits; we "below the liners" fly coach. As the Valium took effect, I fell asleep. I have no idea how long I was out. However, when I awoke I was mortified to find myself severely listing to one side with my head drooping at about chest level of the poor guy sitting next to me. To his credit, he didn't wake me, which was more than I could say for myself had the roles been reversed.

The few weeks that I was in Florida prior to shooting went well. The rehearsals went smoothly; Ron let me know that he was happy with what I was providing, and the production meetings went well too. In addition, it was interesting working with a cast of legendary performers in the twilight of their careers.

There was one major concern of mine that I will refer to as the *Cocoon* box and was completely powerless over. The *Cocoon* box was something that had not been in the original script, but had come up in a discussion I had with Ron prior to leaving for Florida. Its purpose was to warn the aliens of humans approaching and to determine the level of life inside the cocoons. It was only prominently seen a couple of times in the film. The unit appeared to be a dark Plexiglas tower that stood about three feet tall and was powered by a remote-control unit that had two joysticks. The controlling device would be in the hands of Harvey, the fellow I hired to design and build the box. It was to contain several panels that could be electronically opened and closed which would emit different colors and patterns of light. It also had to have the ability to raise and lower itself. The top portion of the box housed a bright flashing light, much like a powerful camera flash. The flash would supposedly be activated when an unauthorized person or non-alien approached.

Although by this time I had three feature films under my belt, there was still plenty to learn, and I learned a potent lesson regarding this box. When the idea of the unit was first discussed, I should have immediately included the film's special effects department. They could have been involved with the design and construction of it. Even if they did not build the box themselves, they could have hired craftsmen they trusted. This would have given them the opportunity to learn how to operate and repair it themselves when we were on location. Not knowing this at the time, I brought Harvey in to meet Ron and discuss the function of the box. The unit was under construction when I left for St. Petersburg.

The first day of shooting was just around the corner, and due to my obsessive work during pre-production, I felt well prepared. Mark and I had gone through the script thoroughly and were very much on the same page and agreed that we had left no stone unturned. However, as a friend of mine so aptly put after years as a prop man when asked if he felt well prepared, "Well... I'm all set to be caught off guard. You never know what might come up unexpectedly." That is a very good way to sum up how we feel a good deal of the time.

One of the things I noticed in terms of the weather in St. Pete was that almost daily at around 4 p.m., it would cloud over and rain like hell for about ten minutes. I'm talking about a complete downpour. Afterward, it would be even hotter and muggier than prior to the rain. It was bad enough that the humidity could be cut with a knife, but the real problem was that all of our equipment would get soaked. We quickly learned to anticipate the rain and cover up whatever we possibly could. There were only the two of us, and we couldn't both leave the set to accomplish this, so something, usually the chairs, would get drenched.

Since that time there have been a couple of changes for the better. There is now an on-set dresser (that position didn't exist back then) who helps us in situations like that because they are considered prop personnel. The primary job of an on-set dresser is to make sure that each piece of the furniture on the set is on its proper mark. Furniture is constantly being moved to accommodate ever-changing camera angles. Another thing that has changed for the better is that when we are on distant location, we are frequently given a local union member to add to our department.

Although I was very pleased with how things were going, I still had the *Cocoon* box on my mind and was calling Los Angeles daily to check on its progress.

Harvey and the box were finally on a plane to Florida. The box wasn't to be filmed in the first couple of weeks of shooting, but by the time Harvey arrived, we were only four or five days out from needing it on camera. Jan, our first assistant director, arranged for a *Cocoon* box demonstration for Ron, along with Richard and Lili Zanuck, our producers.

My prop storage unit (for things I didn't have room for on the prop truck) was located in a motel suite that had been emptied and was directly next door to the hotel where most of the crew stayed. This was where the demonstration was to take place. It was a huge deal because all involved had anxiously been waiting for the box to arrive.

Harvey had the entire first day after he arrived to work on the necessary fine tuning, adjusting, and rehearsing with the box in preparation for the much-anticipated unveiling. At the conclusion of the day's filming, the moment had finally arrived! We all eagerly gathered into the motel room for the demonstration. *Dear God, please let this fucking thing work!* I remember being very nervous, but Harvey had assured me everything was in perfect working order and to stop worrying. Holding my breath, I watched Harvey, remote control in hand, run the box through its paces flawlessly. *Yesss!!* It was a hit and we were a hit!! *What a relief.* Ron, Richard, and Lili were extremely happy with what they witnessed.

Harvey and I popped a celebratory brew, had a toast, laughed, and joked about how great we were. With a last swig of beer, we decided to witness one more time, the brilliance of Harvey's masterpiece. He switched the unit back on, did his final check and hit the remote. THE ENTIRE TOP OF THE BOX WENT UP IN FLAMES! As I watched my career going up in smoke, I realized I had better call the fire department immediately.

The box was in the back bedroom of the motel suite and the phone was in the front room, which was actually a blessing because I couldn't bear to watch what was happening. Within minutes, several fire trucks showed up, lights flashing, sirens wailing. Somehow, while I was making the call, Harvey put the flames out. I was in such a state of panic that to this day I cannot remember him telling me how he did it. In any case, the damage was done. The flash unit was completely fried, and the top of the box had melted. I WAS SCREWED!

Cocoon: Post Flame

After surveying the damage to the box and giving our next move some thought, I decided that there was just one sensible thing to do. I threatened to kill Harvey if the box was not ready to be in front of the camera on the scheduled shoot day. I told him that I didn't care what measures needed to be taken, but to figure it out and to do it fast since shooting was only a couple of days away. Changing a shooting schedule due to a prop not being ready is tantamount to Hari-kari. I had worked far too hard on this film, and having future opportunities to work with this group snatched away was just not an option. I probably would not have been replaced, but my job performance assessment would have taken a serious hit. We left that motel/storage room that night with the smell of burnt box lingering in the air.

Harvey had a huge challenge in front of him and thank God he was up to the task. I didn't see his actual process, but by the time the box was to be put in front of the camera, it was ready and worked as it was designed to do. There had to be some modifications to the melted portion, but they were not detected by anyone, and the flash unit was good as new. I was very lucky to have dodged that bullet. Remember the lesson I talked about earlier? This is it: Collaborate with your special-effects department whenever anything like this comes up.

I made an accidental cameo in this film. I can clearly be seen in one of the most important scenes in the movie. Please rent it and check me out, as it will most likely be my only and most memorable performance. The scene is between Wilford Brimley (the grandfather) and Barret Oliver (the grandson). The two are fishing, and Wilford is explaining to the boy that he will be leaving and never coming back to this planet again. At this poignant juncture, I can be seen nonchalantly strolling through the background, large as life. Unknowingly, after leaving the prop truck to return to set, and lost in thought, I moseyed in, totally oblivious to walking directly into the shot. The camera was on a platform in the water facing the road. When I saw it, my first inclination was to duck, run, or hide—do something so as not to ruin the take. Somehow, I was able to avoid these obvious gaffes in judgment. I continued strolling through the shot, pretending to check my shoe for mud or some such thing, and acting as naturally as possible.

When I heard the word cut, I dashed over to the camera operator and told him what had just occurred. He was an accomplished guy whom I trusted, and he told me not to worry about it. I literally never gave it another thought... until the cast and crew screening of the film several months later. Bigger than life, there I came, right through the shot. Amazingly, no one ever said a word about it. The only people who ever really appreciated it were my friends, who got a hardy laugh out of seeing me just passing through!

The entire cast was easy to work with, which is icing on the cake when it comes to my job, but I particularly enjoyed some funny conversations with Wilford Brimley. I had done a lot of horseback riding, even worked at a rental horse stable as a kid, and Wilford was a ranch owner and real cowboy. Prior to acting, he had worked as a wrangler (a crew member who works specifically with horses and livestock) in the film business and had done some extra work as well, primarily in westerns. Having a common love for horses put me in his good graces from the beginning.

We had several enjoyable talks over the course of the show. Wilford had all sorts of funny cowboy stories and anecdotes that he enjoyed sharing, and I enjoyed hearing. One day, he came to set wearing a shirt he was not particularly fond of provided by the wardrobe department. He walked up to me and said, "Ya know son, if a man had two shirts like this, he could shit on one of 'em and cover it up with the other."

In one scene while walking toward the pool with his two cronies, he adlibbed about an erection he supposedly had as a result of his new energy level from swimming in the pool filled with cocoons: "like blue steel, a cat couldn't scratch it," and my personal favorite, "like a small boy's arm with a peach in his fist." (That one may take a little visualization.) He had several gems like this that he was more than happy to share. Ron liked them, leaving many in the film.

Wilford was friendly enough to the crew with some exceptions, as he didn't care much for authority figures and could be a bit short with them. He hated the walkie-talkies and hearing the chatter that came over them, particularly if it interfered with his preparing for a scene.

Another thing that he was adamant about was not doing close-ups or single shots without the actor he was involved with in the scene doing their lines off camera. When filming close-ups, the scene is performed from beginning to end with the camera focused only on the face of the actor whose close-up is needed. Many times this is done with the script supervisor reading the other character's lines. Stars or lead actors often prefer to leave the set after their close-ups are done, rather than do the scene again, off camera, to help the actors in smaller roles with their close-up shots.

It's harder to give an optimal performance without the actual actor being there but off camera, because so much of what an actor does is react to the other person in the scene, and usually the script supervisor is merely reading the lines with little emotion. So the actor being filmed has to remember how the other actor delivered the lines and pretend to be reacting as in the master shot when both actors were on camera. Watching actors over the years deliver incredible close-up performances under those circumstances has reinforced my respect for their craft and the skills required for their job.

* * *

Maureen Stapleton played Wilford's wife. Maureen, like the rest of the group, was getting up in years and could have been cranky or fussy about our long hours or having to work so many nights, but I never heard a cross word from her. There was one thing, however, that she wasn't crazy about, and that was being out on the small boat we were filming on for several nights. The boat had a slimmed down crew, as the entire cast needed to be on board with several extras as well.

One of Maureen's favorite beverages was champagne. She came to me a few days before we were to head out to open waters and informed me that there was no way she was getting on board "that thing" unless I had two bottles of her favorite brand, chilled and handy. Having experienced DeNiro being too drunk to work, but having had Kazan's okay to provide him with drinks, I knew to check with Ron before sending someone to the liquor store. He wasn't crazy about the idea; however, he probably felt he had no choice in the matter. I have no idea if he had a conversation with her concerning this or not, but in the end, I was to go ahead and get her the bubbly.

Cut to... the boat. The champagne had been given to Maureen in a small cooler upon boarding. She had been indulging throughout the evening and had been fine so far. Now that it was time for her close-up, however, she was sound asleep (passed out) down below. Word got to Ron up on deck. I had a sense of what might be happening and was standing right next to Ron when he received the news. He turned to me, and almost like *Richie Cunningham*, said, "Well, Steve, it looks like Maureen won't be able to answer the bell for this round." It was a classic statement, because he and I are huge sports fans and we talked sports frequently.

Maureen was awakened. She came up to the top deck, and like a stoned Robert Mitchum when the cameras rolled, gave a wonderful performance. Ron got what he needed and she promptly went back down below and resumed her snooze!

Cocoon: Notes

Today I watched the *Cocoon* DVD with Ron's commentary. It brought me back twenty-nine years to the four months I spent in St. Petersburg. Seeing it all again brought back some emotions that haven't surfaced in many years.

The DVD brought back memories of the actors who have now passed on. Wilford, who was really only in his late fifties when the film was shot, is an exception. Mostly, it brought back the feelings I had as a young property master and how much of myself I put into that film. I felt somewhat melancholy hearing Ron's voice describing each scene, reminding me how much I enjoyed working for him.

CHAPTER 9

Pee-wee's Big Adventure

To refresh my memory, since it has been twenty-eight years since *Pee-wee's Big Adventure* was made, I rented the DVD and watched it with my wife. This film was loaded with props, gadgets, and all kinds of off-the-wall stuff, as anyone who has seen a Tim Burton film would expect. The DVD is equipped with a version of the film providing commentary from Paul Reubens, (Pee-wee) and Tim (the director). I liked Paul very much and had a good relationship with Tim as well. Both of these guys are huge talents. Paul was terrific as Pee-wee, a role he later revived on Broadway, and as you know, Tim has gone on to direct several high-budget, high-profile films with tremendous success. His unique style of film making that continues to delight audiences today and Paul's whimsical alter ego were a match made in heaven. They were very savvy to have Danny Elfman do the brilliant musical score as well.

I remember going in for my interview with Tim and how interested he was in hearing about my experiences working with Ron Howard on *Cocoon* and the other films I had worked on. He was easy to talk to, and I got the sense that I would be perfect for this project. He obviously felt the same way as I received a call later that day informing me that I had gotten the job. I had to hit the ground running because the studio had only budgeted for six weeks prep time.

I soon found out just how hard this assignment was going to be because Tim and Paul's vision for the film was going to exceed the budget that Warner Bros. had given me. It quickly became obvious that I had a choice: Give Tim and Paul what they wanted and go over budget, or try to squeak by with what the studio wanted me to spend. One of the most difficult aspects of this job is the fine balance between work you can be proud of, while at the same time pleasing the director (and in this case the star) and not have the studio come down hard on you for over-spending.

Pee-wee: The Bicycle

Pee-wee's bike was like a character in the film. I had a total of fourteen bicycles for the one being portrayed. One of them had to be ready for its close up at any given time and needed to stay in pristine condition. The rest of the bikes were each rigged for specific stunts and gags, or mounted on a trailer so Pee-wee could appear to be riding it while performing silly maneuvers. I also had at least two bikes that he could ride normally. Every bicycle had to match exactly so the audience would think that this *one* bicycle could do all of these amazing things.

Pee-wee: The Budget

One weekend, my home phone rang and it was Tim and Paul on the line. They had been going over the scene in the biker bar to be shot on that Monday and thought it would be a great idea to have breakaway beer pitchers, beer mugs, and beer bottles for Pee-wee to smash during the dance routine he performed to the song, *Tequila,* on the bar top. This was a tall order because it was the weekend and there isn't a place in town that had breakaways that was going to be open until Monday morning. I immediately made some calls and fortunately was able to arrange for a pick up of the items available and have them delivered to set prior to call time.

I think the bill came to about $1,000. Tim and Paul were very pleased that I was able to make this happen. However, the head of production was far less enthused as he was constantly involved in keeping costs down. The minute the bill hit his desk my phone rang. He proceeded to ream me for spending the money without getting his approval first. I told him about the call that I had personally gotten from Tim and Paul over the weekend requesting these items. He couldn't have cared less.

I got a little testy and told him that maybe I should have billed production for my time spent working on the weekend, not to mention the fact that the vendor opened up early for me at no extra charge. Still... no mercy. This is exactly the point I was making at the beginning of this chapter about walking that fine line between the director and production management.

Now having had many more years of experience, I can see the executive's point of view. The money I spend on a project is their responsibility as well, and they deserve to know why and for what the money is being spent. These are things I pay closer attention to today. Having said that, anyone who has seen this film knows that was clearly a standout scene. In fact, when most people hear that I worked on this film, they want to talk about Pee-wee dancing to Tequila on the bar top while smashing the bottles, which explains why in 2008 that scene was nominated for TV Land's Award, "Movie Dance Sequence You Reenacted in Your Living Room."

Pee-wee: The Bikers

Most of the bikers in the bar were the real deal, and one fellow in particular was a member of the most notorious motorcycle club of all. Being a lifelong motorcycle enthusiast, the lifestyle of these guys has always been of interest to me. I won't identify his club affiliation or his name, but I will share a funny story about him. This was the second time I had worked with this guy; the first time was on a biker-themed television pilot that never sold. He had been friends with another crew member I knew from that show, and he invited us both over to his place for a couple of brews after work one day. He had a really cool place in the north San Fernando Valley Mountains and had a collection of old train boxcars on his land.

The place was decorated well and was a perfect biker bachelor pad. He popped open a few beers and checked his answering machine. Message #1 went something like this: "Hi, It's Julie calling; haven't heard back from you; I'm home so give me a call." Message #2: "Hi, Diane here. I'd love to see you again; let's get together soon. Okay?" Message #3: "Hey, it's me Michelle; where are you anyway? Can you come over later?" And this was only the first three... there were several more. He didn't even chuckle about it or return any of their calls while we were there. After all, we had some beer to drink, and these seemed to be the types of calls he got daily anyway. The babes sure do like the bad boys, don't they?

One of the funnier things I heard this grizzled biker say still makes me laugh. He and I were standing near the set talking when another biker walked past with his shirt off, exposing his back and the most amazing mural tattoo I had ever seen. As he walked by, the biker I'm standing with takes a close look at the beautiful artwork on the guy's back. He spits, turns to me, and says, "Fucker's holdin' some baaad stain man."

Pee-wee: The Rodeo and the Stunt Man

There is a rodeo sequence in the film that takes place with Pee-wee supposedly in Texas as he continues the search for his stolen bike. The sequence has him riding a bull. Pee-wee's stunt double on this film was Corey Eubanks. Corey took quite a beating at times, performing some very dangerous stunts. I had gotten to know Corey well and was talking to him while he was stretching just prior to getting on the bull.

He had some rodeo experience in the past but mentioned to me that it had been quite some time since he had actually ridden a bull. Keep in mind this was a real rodeo bull, not a tame, trained animal. My assistant turned to me after he and I had gotten a close look at this beast earlier that day and asked, "What in the world would possess a man to get on one of these things?" I had no sensible answer whatsoever. Once those snot-blowing bastards buck you off, the first thing they try to do is gore you to death.

The time had now come for Corey to mount up. We were ready to roll. I was sitting on the rail just off camera when the chute opened and out they came. It didn't last long. Corey stayed on for about four seconds. I saw the bull kick his hind legs up which lurched Corey forward. At the exact same time the bull swung his head around and their heads collided full on, Corey being the obvious loser. He was knocked out cold, limp as a rag doll and being flopped around with his hand still stuck in the rigging! It was one of the scariest things I had ever seen.

The on-camera clowns were real rodeo clowns and immediately did what they were trained to do—distract the bull and free Corey. Corey lay on the ground motionless as the cowboys ran over to him. *Oh God... please don't let him be dead.* The ambulance standing by raced into the arena and after a few minutes, Corey seemed to regain consciousness, was put on a stretcher, and rushed off to the hospital. Thank God, not long after that, word came to us that he would be okay.

One of the cowboys first on the scene while Corey was lying there in the arena was a character I had known for many years by the name of Dave Rodgers. Dave had been a bareback bronc rider and had later become a wrangler in the film industry. When things settled down a bit, I went over to him to see what he had to say. Cowboys have their own lingo and Dave responded with that cowboy drawl of his, "Well... when ah got ta Corey, he was a snorin' now. That bull reeeely warped eem." I suppose that's as good of an explanation as any.

Corey was back in action in a couple of days all set to get the shit knocked out of him the next time a stunt came around. Such is the life of a Hollywood stunt man. By retirement time, most of them have permanent limps, enough screws in their bodies to need a note from a doctor to get past the surveillance screening at the airport, and a few other long-term physical issues too.

They are a close-knit wild group of folks who hang together and have lots of fun, but when the cameras roll, it's strictly business, because without careful planning any stunt could be their last.

In my opinion, *Pee-wee's Big Adventure* is a film classic. Other than constantly being questioned about my spending by the studio heads, it was truly an exciting project to work on and rates high on the list of films that I am most proud to have been a part of. The film can be enjoyed again and again and you will probably notice something new every time. For my part, I am glad I sided with Tim and Paul and gave them what they wanted.

CHAPTER 10

Property Master vs. the Set Decorator

If you are interested in the inner workings of the art/prop/ set decorating departments, I think this chapter will be of interest to you. This portion of the book gives you an important look at the dynamics between the set decorator and the property master and how the production designer figures into the equation.

First of all, it is critical to clearly understand the difference between these integral departments. The production designer, the set decorator, the property master, and their crews make up the art department. It's not just the general public that has no idea what our various responsibilities are, but many of the on-set crew members *not* in the art department have no clue either! This may be hard to believe, but it is the absolute truth. I have had grips, electricians, sound people, you name it, who have been in the business for years ask me, "Where did you get that couch? I love it!" or, "Can you tell me where I can purchase that painting?" These items are the responsibility of the set decorator, *not* the property master. It amazes me how little each department knows about the other departments.

In terms of the art department, the production designer has the responsibility of the overall look of the show. The production designer is like an architect, designing sets that the construction department will then build on a sound stage. He/she may also select existing location choices for the director to choose from. For example: Existing locations such as functioning restaurants, grocery stores, or even a privately owned home are known as practical locations. The designer may love the structure of a home or the scenic overlook, but will have the set decorator gut the existing furniture and "dress" (put into) the set, furniture that is more appropriate for the character that is supposedly living there.

Let us assume the film is about a real estate development company. The production designer determines the entire look of the office set: designs the company's logo, decides the layout in terms of where the receptionist would sit, where the security area is, where the elevators are placed, and chooses the carpeting, the wallpaper, where the hanging light fixtures would be and so on. The designer conveys the style and look he or she is trying to achieve to the set decorator, who picks the furniture to dress into the set: the desks and chairs, the pictures on the walls, the table lamps, the computer monitors, and all of the things to personalize the desks such as family photos, plants, whatever best enhances what he/she and the production designer have in mind. They obviously work very closely together and must have a good working relationship.

The production designer, in most cases, chooses the set decorator for the project. When I started in the industry and for several years after that, when a property master was to be decided upon and the director did not have a particular person in mind, the producer or the production manager would bring in people to be interviewed by the director. As the industry has evolved, the production designer choosing the property master has replaced this practice in most instances. Interestingly enough, I have lost jobs when the production designer has requested me, but was overruled by the producer, and also lost out when the producer wanted me but was overruled by the production designer. *Sometimes it's difficult to figure out just where it is best to have one's nose buried.*

Since you know the basic job descriptions for the designer and decorator and at this point you are familiar with the prop master's responsibilities, let me explain where the problems arise between the set decorator and the prop department.

The classic example is that a scene calls for a family dinner with six people. The set decorator supplies the dinnerware (they like to choose this themselves), and we supply the food and drink. Keep in mind that the re-setting of props has to be carefully planned and done as quickly as possible; otherwise the assistant director will be breathing down our necks. It is their responsibility to complete the entire day's scheduled shooting, so you can imagine how they react to a slow re-set of props.

Back to the example, the scene calls for everyone to dig in and begin filling their plates. At any time during that scene or at its conclusion, the director will yell, "CUT! Let's go again!" Directors want the re-set of the food to happen instantly to keep the actors focused and in character. Take two now needs everyone to again have clean plates, drink glasses, and so on. We always ask the decorator for *twelve* dinner plates for a scene with *six* people, because that saves us the time of having to wash and dry them between takes. If we have twelve plates, six can be cleaned during take two, so they are ready to be placed on the table for the take three, if needed. The decorator, more often than not, will leave us short of something, like giving us eight plates and two extra glasses which slows the re-set. When the assistant director starts asking, "Is props ready?" (usually *way* before it is humanly possible), it's very awkward to respond with, "We *would* be if the decorator had left us the proper amount of dinnerware." So... we suck it up and don't say anything.

Here are some other examples that can be frustrating when they occur: a toaster is dressed into the set but without being checked to see if it actually works (which is why I always have a functioning toaster on the truck); extra sheets or pillow cases are not left for the bed, when it is a given that the actor's make-up will soil them; not enough extra candles are supplied for the candelabra when the scene calls for them to be lit; ashtrays are forgotten for a set where smoking takes place; or they put pen holders on a desk with no pens in them; an actor goes to a filing cabinet looking for a specific file (which is our responsibility), but no other files have been dressed into the cabinet; a guy opens his desk drawer to pull out his gun (which we provide) but the drawer is completely empty of anything else. A good decorator will take the time to dress in items that should be in that drawer.

To be fair, some set decorators are very conscientious about these things, but the list above is comprised of actual occurrences that I have experienced, even though I have had discussions with the decorator pertaining to these very issues well in advance of shooting. When problems due to these oversights occur, the prop people are subject to taking the heat because a) the set decorators are rarely on set or b) many directors don't realize that those things are the decorator's responsibility, not ours. I always try to visit the upcoming sets to be certain that these details have been handled, but occasionally time won't allow for that.

I am certain that this goes both ways and that a well-versed decorator would be able to cite examples of prop people they feel could use some additional schooling. You can now see how important the right prop master/set decorator combination is in order to have a smooth-running art department.

CHAPTER 11

Jumpin' Jack Flash

In 1987 I received an offer to take over a show that was approximately three weeks into shooting. It was awkward for me because I had not prepared the show, and the departing property master had an entirely different system than mine. I kept his assistant so that I would have someone who knew what was going on and had a sense of continuity. I also brought in my assistant, Mark, who had been with me on *Cocoon*.

The film starred Whoopi Goldberg, who was really fun to work with if you were a crew member. She may have been tougher on producers in terms of creative decisions, but my dealings with her all went smoothly.

Coming in at this stage did not allow me the opportunity to get to know our director Penny Marshall, (it is during the pre-production period that ideas are bandied about and relationships are formed), which may be why I never felt that comfortable in my dealings with Penny. While not actually shooing me away when I approached her with questions or ideas, she seemed to not take my involvement seriously. Not exactly what I had hoped for from Laverne (Penny Marshall played Laverne on the TV series, *Laverne and Shirley*). This was simply my experience with her, which may be quite different from those who work with her on a regular basis.

I had worked for Joel Silver (the producer) prior to this on a series starring the late Patrick Swayze entitled *The*

Renegades. He had been happy with my work so when my name came up to be the replacement, he approved.

In spite of my late arrival on this film, I kept things running smoothly until one unfortunate incident. Apparently this one thing was so unforgivable, I would never hear from Joel Silver again.

The unfortunate incident involved automatic weapons gunfire that worked in tandem with a huge plate-glass window being shattered by our effects department. I rented all of the film's weapons, as I always had without any problem, from a well-known armory used by many property masters. That's normally where my involvement ends—making sure that the proper firepower is ordered and shows up on time—because although I am licensed to rent and use certain weapons, I am not licensed to carry or use fully automatic weapons. Weapons of this nature require someone who carries a special safe in their vehicle. The armorer must also know how to break these weapons down, repair or clean them on the spot, and be fully educated in all aspects of these very dangerous weapons. Even though blank ammunition is being fired, they are still capable of causing serious injury or death and require a licensed expert to be in attendance when being used.

Unfortunately, the weapons brought to set for this particular scene kept jamming and caused delays in shooting. Being the property master, I was responsible for this mess and endured quite a tongue lashing from Joel in front of an entire audience of crew members. It was horrible!

As Joel had done several "shoot 'em up" films, he knew of a company that he would have preferred to use but never shared that information with me. In retrospect, perhaps I should have discussed this with him before placing the order. I have no problem defending myself if I have a leg to stand on, but in this case there was really nothing I could say. I had chosen the company to do the job, and they failed to do the job well. I took my verbal abuse, and that was the end of it.

A few weeks later, we had night shooting in downtown Los Angeles with only two scenes to complete. We had a six p.m. call and should have had no problem finishing by sunup. There was nothing difficult in the first scene that would slow the shoot down: kids, dogs, or stunts. It was a simple dialogue scene.

The second, and more difficult, scene was a car stunt. The stunt driver was to gain speed and flip the vehicle by running up a pipe ramp. This device is a thick pipe that gradually rises to about a forty-five degree angle. The driver gets up to speed and runs one side of the car up the ramp, which causes it to flip. Stunts take a long time to properly set up.

The night was progressing and Penny continued to shoot take after take with the dialogue scene. *What the hell is going on here? We still need to do a stunt that takes time to set up, rehearse, and have cameras properly placed. Why is no one else getting concerned about this?* Sure enough, when they finished the dialogue scene, the rush was on to get the stunt shot before the sun came up. Rushing into a stunt increases the odds that something will go wrong.

The car to be flipped is totally reinforced with a steel cage so when it lands on its roof or its sides, it won't cave in. Several cameras are used for a stunt such as this, because it can only be shot once and must be covered from several different angles. As we were getting closer to sunrise, things were getting more and more chaotic.

The cameras were finally in place, the driver was belted into his seat, and it appeared that everything was ready to go. But at the last minute, there was a discrepancy about the position of one of the cameras. The discussion was whether or not the camera should be farther away from where the front of the car was supposed to stop, or if it was okay to leave it where it was in order to obtain the best shot possible. Due to time running out, the quick decision was made. It was fine to leave it in its current position. The assistant director made sure all was set, checked with the stunt driver, and got the thumbs up. I then heard, "Roll Cameras... Action!" I was standing at a safe distance but with a clear view.

The car picked up speed as it headed toward the ramp, the driver positioning it to flip. It flew up the ramp, flipped, and landed violently on its roof, sparks flying—and KABOOM—still going about thirty miles per hour, hit the camera that had been in question.

The camera shattered into a million pieces and actually had to be carried away in a cardboard box. The other cameras got their shots and the stunt driver was fine. Had they budgeted their time properly, more thought would have been given to the cameras' placements and this might have been avoided.

In closing this chapter, I would like to write about a very talented and funny man who was taken from this world far too early. Phil Hartman was a character in *Jumpin' Jack Flash*, but I had already known him from my days on *Pee-wee's Big Adventure*. Phil, along with Pee-wee and another writer by the name of Michael Varlhol were the writers of that hilarious film. Phil was such a pleasant and entertaining fellow and so much fun to have on set. He was a brilliant comedian and impressionist. My favorite impression was Jack Benny. He would transform into Jack right in front of your eyes. He could brighten the mood by just being onset. Phil was one of those people that had that special something and is profoundly missed.

CHAPTER 12

Smooth Criminal

During the mid 1980's I was asked to do a video starring Michael Jackson. *Smooth Criminal* was a song on his upcoming album, *Bad*. Shortly after being hired I saw Michael for the first time. He was with a group of about four or five people and was wearing a jacket similar to the style the Beatles wore on the *Sgt. Pepper's* album, and a surgical mask. I felt a bit star struck at that moment. After all, this was one of the world's most beloved stars.

We were going to be shooting on a stage in Culver City, California, that back then was known as Laird Studio, which originally was The Desilu Studio (owned by and named after Desi and Lucy). Coincidently, *Smooth Criminal* was shot on the same stage that I had been on for *Airplane* back in 1979.

Bodyguards always accompanied Michael. I don't recall any of their names except for Miko Brando, Marlon's son, who was with Michael until the very end. Normally for A-list stars, motor homes are used as dressing rooms and places to chill out. These are parked near the stage entrance. I never really got a good look at any of the motor homes for Michael or his entourage because an outdoor enclosure constructed with thirty-foot walls surrounded them. This enclosure was called "The Compound", and had a bodyguard stationed at the entrance at all times. The main man in charge of Michael's security team had been with him since he was a child and also served as Michael's driver.

The only people I ever saw close to him other than his guards were Colin Chilvers, our director; his manager, Frank DiLeo; his hair and makeup specialist, Karen Faye (also with Michael until he passed); his personal wardrobe attendant; and Bob Dunn, Michael's animal trainer, who brought Michael's chimpanzee named "Bubbles" to the set periodically.

We as general crew members were asked not to talk to Michael. If contact became necessary, it was to be communicated through his wardrobe man. There were a couple of things that needed clarification for me in terms of props, and instead of simply asking Michael, I had to ask the wardrobe guy, who would ask Michael for me, and then relay the message back.

Michael would occasionally have a child from the "Make a Wish Foundation" come to set to meet him. This is a wonderful foundation allowing terminally ill children a final wish. When a child chose to meet Michael, he or she would come to set with parents, family members, or nurses. Michael's wardrobe man would come to me and say, "Michael would like for you to set up some chairs for his guests," which of course we were happy to do. He would spend time with the child and family; and when they left, we would fold the chairs and put them away, at which time the wardrobe guy would come back and say, "Michael said to say 'Thank you' for the chairs."

One thing I will say about him is that he appeared to be a very decent person, always taking time out for children wanting to meet him. I brought my kids to the set when they were about five and six and asked the wardrobe guy if Michael would say hello to them. Michael actually came over, sat with them for a few minutes, and gave each of them an autographed picture. In those few minutes, they spoke to Michael more than I did for the entire time I was with him on set.

It was fun to watch Michael work with the dancers in the video. It beat watching a boring dialogue scene or having to prop a huge sequence with 200 extras. Michael was absolutely amazing to watch and had assembled a group of extremely talented dancers.

During the entire dance portion of the video, the special effects guys would pump the stage full of what appeared to be fog, a look that many directors and cameramen love. Supposedly the fog had been approved as being safe for us to breathe, since for weeks we would all be exposed to it. Interestingly enough, Michael never wore his surgical mask inside the stage at all. The times I saw him wearing it he was outside. There were several large fans inside the stage, and as time went on I observed a black gooey substance beginning to form on the blades. I could only assume that the fog approved for us to breathe was responsible for the goo buildup.

Gregory Peck showed up on stage one night to visit with Michael. I remember him sitting there in a director's chair, observing the evening's work. He was probably the most striking and regal looking man I have ever seen. He was impeccably dressed and wore an ascot around his neck, truly one of Hollywood's most famous leading men.

One night while shooting on the back lot of Universal Studios, our first assistant director shouted to the crew over a loudspeaker to immediately stop what we were doing and head toward the nearest exit. I had no idea what it was all about. Safely assembled outside the property, the entire crew was informed that there had been a bomb threat.

Universal Studios is known for the tours they provide daily, which is a large source of their profits. Apparently, a tour guide had informed a tram full of visitors that Michael Jackson was starring in a video that was taking place on the studio's back lot, where the tram had just passed. One of the visitors evidently thought it would be funny to phone in a threat that a bomb was going to go off near our set. As I recall, it took an hour or so to determine that it was a hoax before we were allowed to return to work.

Several years later, on the day that Michael died, I was driving my hybrid car to the set of the show I was working on at the time. Suddenly, for the first and only time ever, it lost power and I was forced to pull over to the side of the road. It was very strange. After a few moments, it restarted with no trouble. When I arrived at location, I was told that Michael had been rushed to a hospital and had likely died. Later, when the news reported Michael's approximate time of death, I realized a chilling coincidence; it was very close to the time that my car had lost power. I obviously don't know what caused my car to quit like that, but could it be... ???

CHAPTER 13

Losing Out on *Driving Miss Daisy* and *Parenthood*

As can happen to anyone in this industry, I was left out in the cold back in 1986. I had been hired for a film entitled, *50,* starring Richard Dreyfuss and Elliot Gould, being directed by Mark Rydell of *On Golden Pond.* I don't know all the details, but this film had at one time been in the late planning stages when for some reason, it fell through and wasn't made. Now, *50* resurfaced and had all the makings of a hit film.

It was early in the pre-production phase when I received a call from Ron Howard's office offering me the opportunity to do the film, *Parenthood. Shit, no way can I leave the film I just started. I would definitely be burning a bridge.* I hated to let it go but I had no choice. To make matters worse, a few days later, I received a call from Richard and Lili Zanuck offering me *Driving Miss Daisy.*

50 was a project many property masters would have loved to do, and I was happy to have gotten it, but it did hurt to turn down people that I respected, liked, and had worked with before. However, it appeared I had a project that was shaping up to be a winner. The film was to begin shooting in New York City and then come back to Los Angeles to continue filming. I've always loved New York and was looking forward to going. I had done all the prep work I could do in Los Angeles, and it was time to head east to work with the assistant that had been lined up for me.

My assistant in New York was a fellow by the name of Michael Badalucco (the author of the Foreword to this book.) He was a perfect fit, a New York Italian guy with a great sense of humor who knew the town like the back of his hand. Michael had plenty of experience as he had worked for the well-known New York property master, Jimmy Mazzola, for several years. He not only did everything I had asked of him before I had arrived, but at lunch or after work he would show me great places to eat, drink, or take in an off-Broadway show, often joining me for the occasion. We had fun while getting our work done and became fast friends.

There is one story that I still enjoy sharing with people. It was our first day working together and Michael was driving me around town to pick up some props for which he had arranged while I was still in Los Angeles. For those of you who know New York, you know what driving is like in that town, and of course there is never anywhere to park, particularly for making brief stops. Michael pulled up to Hammacher Schlemmer (a department store) and chose to double-park to enable him to quickly run in and make our pick up.

As he got out of the car, I felt like he was deserting me and began to feel a bit panicked because being double-parked and blocking a lane in New York City is like begging for a confrontation by any number of people... not to mention the NYPD. I yelled, "Michael, what are you doing? You can't just leave me sitting here like this! What if someone comes up and hassles me; what am I supposed to tell them?" Without a second's hesitation, Michael responded as he bounded toward the entrance, "Tell them to go fuck themselves!!!!" *Oh yeah, of course, what was I thinking? This is New York!*

Michael had mentioned to me that being a prop man was really not a permanent thing for him. Actually he was an actor with no well-known credits yet. To be honest, I really didn't give that too much thought at the time, but was very pleasantly surprised when years later Michael won an Emmy Award for his portrayal of "Jimmy Berluti" on the very successful series, *The Practice,* that ran for several seasons. He has also appeared in many feature films as well as a host of other roles on television. I'm truly happy for him. I have only seen Michael a handful of times over the years, but he is a close friend of a good friend of mine, so periodically I do see him and his lovely wife, Brenda.

Things were coming together for me in the Big Apple, and I was having fun. Suddenly it didn't bother me so much to have had to turn down *Parenthood* and *Driving Miss Daisy*. But... my good fortune was about to come to a screeching halt. After another good day of work, I was summoned to the producer's office. *What can this be about? It can't be good.* I was told the director and star were having creative differences and we were officially on hold. I was to wait for further instruction that would be coming soon.

The instruction *did* come soon. We were to pack up and return to Los Angeles. The word was we would begin shooting in L.A. and come back to New York for the last few weeks of shooting. I never really bought into that story and in fact none of it happened. The film was canceled for the second and final time. What this meant for me was, no *Parenthood*, no *Driving Miss Daisy*, and in fact... no job at all.

CHAPTER 14

Havana

The Sydney Pollack film, starring Robert Redford, was going to be lucrative but would last eleven months and would prove to be an extremely difficult endeavor and one of the most horrendous experiences of my career, if not my life.

The first problem with working on *Havana* was that it was to be filmed entirely on location in the Dominican Republic. Once again my work would take me away from my home and children, who were now seven and eight years old. When they were younger, it was far less disruptive to their education and routine to bring them on location. Because that wasn't going to be possible on this project, I would be separated from them for a long time.

I try to recall what was going through my mind when I took this assignment. Was I simply following in the footsteps of my father who was absent during my formative years? Was I so out of touch with my feelings that I didn't realize how much I loved my kids and how hard it would be to be apart from them? I look back now, and it seems as if I was sleeping through my existence, existing but not being in touch with the reality that was my life. How could I convince myself that it was okay to leave a seven-year-old little girl and an eight-year-old little boy for such a long period of time? The moments I missed with them at that age can never be recovered, and I will always regret the choices I made at that point in my life.

I had a meeting with the producers, signed my deal, and was now the property master on 1991's largest budget film. After I accepted this project, the next year my life was a nightmare, beginning with my first meeting with Sydney, where I was whisked away from the production office with the producer in a golf cart to the back lot of Universal Studios where Sydney's offices were located.

Sydney was unfriendly from the start and had that aura about him that says: *I am the Almighty and you are way out of your element to be in my presence.* When I entered his office and sat down, Sydney looked at me and asked, "What assurance do I have that you are capable of doing this job?" *Oh man...* I had a sinking feeling at that moment, but I had already committed to the project. My response was that he was more than welcome to check with any of the people involved in the films I had already done, and perhaps that would give him some assurance. He spent the next fifteen minutes or so making me feel as uncomfortable as possible and when he finished, he had me shuttled back to my office. *Great, this is gonna be fun.*

For the next few weeks, I researched, gathered, and studied information on Havana, Cuba in 1958 so I could be as accurate as possible with my props. Fidel Castro was making his way with his army toward the city with his closest associate, Che Guevera, at his side. Up until that time, Batista had been in power, and Cuba was a huge playground for wealthy Americans to gamble, party, and find beautiful women. There were epic-sized stage shows, burlesque shows, and extravagances of all types, like Vegas on steroids. I knew I needed to back up my props with documented research, as "The Syd Monster" would constantly challenge me. Having already done several films by this time but nothing on this scale, I with maniacal diligence—probably as much out of fear as anything else—did what I believed to be a stellar job of preparation.

We received word that Sydney wanted to have a meeting with the costume designer (Sydney's brother, Bernie), the producer, and myself, so Sydney could get some insight into how our preparation was coming along. We put together a presentation including research materials, photographs, historical clippings and the like, to show him how busy and thorough we were with our pre-production efforts. Bernie was a well-known costume designer and had been Redford's dresser for years. I had heard Sydney wasn't confident in his own brother, even though he had been a successful costume designer for several other well-established stars.

As the meeting began, Sydney called on Bernie to present some of his research material first. Bernie laid out a well-prepared presentation for Syd and said, pointing to some of his photographs and sketches, "Well, Sydney, I think this would be a good idea for...." That was as far as he got when Sydney looked up at him and said in a nasty tone, "A good idea for *what*, Bernie?" Poor Bernie didn't even get the chance to finish a sentence before Sydney jumped all over him. As I recall, he was not impressed with anything he saw from either of us. At this point, I was getting the idea that my immediate future was not looking too bright. What an understatement!

I came away from that meeting knowing that there was only one way to survive. Sydney needed to see and approve *every single possible prop* before we left for Santo Domingo. I knew that acquiring things there would be substantially different than acquiring things in the States.

As I already stated, it is common practice to show directors the important props before they are used on set. I could see that with Sydney, even that might not be enough. Keep in mind that this was a very prop-heavy show. Not only were all the props period pieces, on many days we used 100 to 300 extras, many of which needed to have the appropriate props as well.

Let us now go to my first visit to the Dominican Republic, which took place about six weeks into my preparation period. There were several reasons for this trip: for me to get a sense of the area, to see what might be available to purchase or obtain there as opposed to bringing from Hollywood, to find a caterer capable of supplying the on-camera banquets and food scenes, to interview local help who were bilingual and capable of learning quickly and able to follow orders.

We had been briefed about etiquette and some of the dangers of being in a third-world country. Drugs of any type were to be strictly avoided. Many of the construction crew had been brought to the Dominican Republic from England, and unfortunately one of them got too drunk one night. He was apprehended purchasing cocaine and was taken to the prison somewhere on the island. The word was that the prison was absolutely frightening. The prisoners ran the joint, and the guards patrolled only the outer limits. You can imagine what this poor guy went through in there. He was there for at least six months before the company was able to find a way to get him out. I heard he wasn't in too good of shape when he was released, but I never saw him before or after his incarceration. The only thing I do know for sure is that he was there, and it was miserable.

The day after arriving in Santa Domingo I set out to do my work. I was assigned an English-speaking driver who was to take me to places that I wanted to see. What stood out in my research were vendors driving around in beaten pick-up trucks, loaded down with fruit to sell. The on-camera vehicles are the responsibility of the transportation department, but any signage on the vehicle or anything dressed onto the vehicle, like fruit, vegetables, or any other items, fall under the auspices of the prop department. I decided to ask my driver to start out by taking me to a place where I would be able to purchase large quantities of fruit. The first thing I discovered was that my driver did not speak English any better than I could speak Spanish. *Oh well—might as well get used to this.* It was obviously going to be an ongoing issue.

This was to be my first glimpse into what was coming my way. I had never been in a third-world country prior to this. I had been all over the United States; I had been in Argentina and parts of Mexico; but the sights, sounds and smells of my new environment were completely foreign to me. To begin with, smoke billowed into the air from incinerators and mounds of junk. Where there was construction, the tools were mostly hand tools as opposed to the sophisticated machinery used in the States. There were street vendors selling everything from chickens to candy to fast food. There were hordes of young men trying to wash car windshields whenever there was a stop in traffic. Due to a shortage of power, roving blackouts affected portions of the city daily. The largest vehicle at any intersection was the vehicle that had the right-of-way. I even saw a family of three cruising down the road on a Honda 50 Step-through model from the 60's. Nice homes and neighborhoods transitioned into areas dominated with clapboard houses. Many of the streets were not paved. Small mom-and-pop businesses left their storefronts wide open to deal with the nonstop sweltering heat. Power lines hung dangerously low.

When we finally arrived at the fruit market, it was absolutely amazing and bizarre at the same time. Visualize an acre or more of fruit vendors and what seemed like a hundred small and severely beaten pickup trucks so loaded down with fruit that one more banana seemed likely to topple them onto their sides. I remember an abundance of activity with the buying and selling of fruit by men wearing the most threadbare clothing I had ever seen. I took photos for research purposes, and then it was time to move on to our next location. There was a problem, however.

We were driving through an extremely poor section of town. The residences were put together with old boards, corrugated metal, chicken wire, and whatever else would hold them up. None of the toddlers wore any clothes. People were sort of milling about, some carrying jugs of water, some just sitting around doing whatever they could to stay as cool as possible. I remember thinking, *I hope I'm safe around here,* as I had only just met my non-English-speaking driver that day and was in an area that could only be described as desperate.

The warnings we had been given about being in this country were circling in my head just a moment before it happened. Our van suddenly broke down right in the middle of that Godforsaken neighborhood. I had a pocketful of American money and was wearing a Rolex watch my father had given me for my thirty-third birthday. Not being the most positive thinker, my first thought was, *I'm going to die now.* I popped the watch off of my wrist and put it in my pocket. I asked the driver what he thought had happened to the van but he just shrugged, like, "I don't know."

There we sat, steam pouring out from under the hood as the townsfolk began approaching our disabled vehicle. Visions of my children kept coming to mind, as I believed I would never see them again. I sat there, frozen. More and more villagers came over as my driver hopped out of the van and began talking with them. The next thing I know, there are men looking under the hood and bringing jugs of water over. Instead of being dragged out of the van and beaten to death, as I was sure was about to happen, it appeared as if they were working on the van trying to get us moving again. That is exactly what happened. They got the thing running in about fifteen minutes, and we were off. I used my best Spanish to thank them before letting my driver know that I had had enough for one day, and to get me back to the hotel as quickly as possible—thank you very much!

The next few days consisted of, among other things, finding a caterer for my on-camera food. The woman that was referred to me quoted a price twenty times what I ultimately paid. I think she thought that since Hollywood was coming to town she might as well tap into the cash cow, but what she didn't realize was that I had done my homework and had researched approximately what the price should be. When I received her bid, I laughed and tossed it into the *basura* (that's Spanish for trash).

I had seen in my research that I needed adult-sized tricycles equipped with oversized baskets used by many vendors in Cuba. I found a bicycle dealer who was able to build the bikes that I needed. The problem with having things done in the Dominican Republic was trying to get across that the product was needed by a specific date. Since the Dominicans I was dealing with knew nothing about the stresses of filmmaking and tended to work on their own schedule, this got to be a bit scary at times. Ultimately, the tricycles were finished on time, but I decided it would cause far less worry to have as much as I could shipped from home.

My team was to consist of Glenn, my assistant from Los Angeles; Jimmy from Florida, who had been with me on *Cocoon 2*; and at least one full-time Dominican assistant. I interviewed three bilingual locals, two women and one young man, settling initially on one of the girls. Jimmy didn't like the girl I chose, but as it turns out she was fully capable of being the on-camera prop-food caterer, so I gave her that position. The other girl ended up being hired by the caterer that provides meals for the crew, so our full-time local prop person wound up being Fidel, the young man I had interviewed. Fidel had not interviewed as well as the girls; however, he turned out to be the best suited for us. Once I gained confidence in Fidel's ability and grew to know him, I nicknamed him "Fidleman" (pronounced FY-dull-man) due to my Jewish upbringing.

By the time I returned to L.A. to continue my prep work, I had secured my crew, found a caterer, ordered my three-wheel bicycles, and learned where to find large quantities of fruit. I also had a better idea of what props I would be able to procure while in the D.R.

Now that I was back home for a few final weeks of prep, my job was to acquire the props still needed and have them shipped to Santo Domingo. My main concern upon leaving was not so much about how well I had prepared for the job—I felt pretty good about that. The question in my mind was, how difficult was it going to be to deal with Sydney on a daily basis for that length of time?

It didn't take long to find out!

Havana: The Riot

As you know by now, a crucial part of supplying a good-looking prop involves aging it appropriately. Like wardrobe, if a prop is supposed to appear used, it should not look like it just came out of a package or a box. Can you imagine watching a western and some sod buster rides into town on his horse after being out on the range for a month or so, and his hat looks like it's straight off the shelf of a Western store? So it is with props.

Since my research had shown street vendors cooking by the side of the road, and it had been incorporated into the extras' breakdown supplied by the assistant director's department, we now had to come up with several pots, pans, and assorted cooking utensils that looked like they had been through years of use over open fires with jury-rigged grates.

Aging props can be tricky. We (Jimmy, Glenn, and myself) came up with an idea that we were certain would solve our dilemma. Unfortunately, Fidleman was off on other errands or he would have surely warned us about our brainstorm. Our idea was to purchase a large supply of brand-new cooking utensils from the *fereteria* (hardware store) and go to any neighborhood in Santo Domingo to trade our new stuff for old with the locals. Great idea; right?

We loaded our van with a large supply of brand-new cooking gear. Our not-so-good-English-speaking driver, Felipe, didn't have a clue about what we were up to. We headed out to find a place to trade our wares.

It didn't take us long to find just the spot. We saw some street vendors busily grilling up a storm. We stopped and showed them a small sample of our new cookware, and with limited Spanish and lots of hand gesturing, were able to convey our trading plan to them. At first, it worked like a charm. They couldn't believe their good fortune. Not a one of them had ever seen or heard of anything quite like this. We opened the side door to our van and let them select new items that most resembled the older goods they had been using.

Suddenly, I noticed the crowd was beginning to grow and the speed at which the trading was taking place was accelerating. (Picture the episode with Lucy and Ethel trying to box the chocolates.) We tried to keep up, but soon it became apparent that the crowd was now getting out of control. By the time I realized this, and alerted my guys to the emerging problem, it was too late. The frenzy was on! We managed to get back into the van, but it was not possible to close the windows because of the arms that were reaching through trying to grab what they could. We couldn't close the van doors for the same reason.

We now had to aggressively push as many of them out as we could and yelled to Felipe to get going. We began moving slowly, due to the amount of people coming toward us from all directions, and we finally succeeded in closing the doors and windows. When I looked out the rear of the van, I watched as more and more people chased us down the street waving their old cookware, trying to get us to stop and trade.

As we began to pick up a little momentum, the crowd continued to follow with an ever-increasing sense of urgency. Once again, the situation took an ominous turn... WE CAME TO A DEAD END! *Holy shit!!* We were now completely trapped. A sea of faces and hands pressed up against our windows and the van began rocking.

Like the feeling I had when the van broke down on the first day of my visit, I feared I would never again see my children. I barked orders for Felipe to very carefully put the van in reverse and slowly back up. The last thing I wanted was for anyone to get hurt, but at the same time I was focused on getting out of there alive. The next several minutes were very intense, but we were able to force our way free.

It may have been a frightening situation, but we came away with an ample supply of aged cookware. We did it—and lived to tell about it too. Mission accomplished!

Havana: The Ferry

The first several days of shooting were on sets built inside of a warehouse. One of the sets was the interior of the ferry, and another one was the portion of the ferry where the cars were parked for the trip into Havana. It was on about shoot day number three that we were filming a scene in which Redford finds a military radio hidden in the door panel of a car. Sydney had already approved the radio in an earlier meeting. He had also approved the different styles of license plates that were to be mounted onto the cars. The plates were all specific to the period, including the Cuban plates which had to not only be custom made, but also had to be manufactured specifically with a different style of lettering and numbering that was unique to Cuba during that time period. Syd had a camera mounted on a dolly in such a way as to slowly pan across the front bumpers of the cars to show all of the different locations people had come from to visit Havana.

Suddenly, I heard, "STEVE!" He yelled out in front of the whole crew, "The license plates look like shit and the rest of the props had better start looking a whole lot better than these plates do!" *Ouch.* Keep in mind that these are the very same license plates that he liked when I had shown them to him on a different day.

This is one of the problems with being in the prop or wardrobe departments. We are not working with technical equipment, which puts us at a disadvantage by making things very subjective. At this stage of my career, it didn't occur to me that the person criticizing me might be wrong. Instead, I took all the blame on myself. It took me many years to grasp that important fact. When this type of incident occurs, it is important to examine if there was something that you could have done better, or was this a flare up by an unreasonable person? It takes a thick skin to be in this business and know when to not take things personally and let them roll off your back. It's a good lesson for life in general. I was given several opportunities to begin to grasp this lesson during the filming of *Havana*.

Our next portion of work after the interior ferry sequence was the scene with the cars exiting the ferry and entering Havana. In my entire career, the only sequence that comes close to the enormity of this sequence was the one involving the viewing stands on *Apollo 13*.

The exterior ferry sequence had at least 200 extras and 50 to 75 vehicles. The extras included tourists, dockworkers, military personnel, street vendors, and government officials checking passports. Some of the props we supplied for the tourists included period cameras, luggage, maps, cigarettes, cigars, sunglasses, and hand fans. We loaded up the dock workers with large stevedore dollies bogged down with crates and steamer trunks. For the military, we supplied their rifles and utility belts containing pistols, radios, canteens, and other supplies. We outfitted the street vendors with lottery boards, food items, gum, candy, and cigarettes. To top it off it was at least 95 degrees and very humid.

Jimmy, Glenn, Fidleman, and myself were working the set for this sequence. We were at least two prop people short for this amount of extras, and the prop truck was parked farther from set than any of the other trucks and located down a steep hill. We knew this was going to be a challenge, but we felt up to the task. This sequence took three days to shoot. I hope some of you see this film, because our stuff looked great. I was so proud of my department. It was truly the most challenging three days of work I had ever had; and when the job was completed, we were absolutely whipped. I had blisters on each of my toes and felt like I had been drained of every last bit of energy. We had concluded this portion of the shoot and I was not only relieved but also elated to have come through it so well. That feeling lasted for all of about thirty seconds. I was sitting on the tailgate of the prop truck massaging my aching feet when my assistant Jimmy called for me. I headed back up the hill. He said, "Steve, Sydney wants to talk to you. I think he wants to congratulate you on how great everything looked!" *Awesome. Maybe the guy has an ounce of appreciation in him after all.*

What actually happened was, unbeknownst to us, as we thought the sequence was completed, Syd had decided to grab a last-minute shot of a street vendor, an old man standing by his homemade wooden box on a rickety stand displaying cigarettes, gum, and the likes which he had for sale. I had seen this cool old box on the street during the prep period three to four weeks prior to shooting. An actual Dominican street vendor made his living with it, so it was clearly authentic. It had a great look that caught my eye and I knew at some point, it would come in handy for us to use as a prop. I paid the man three times what it was worth. We took out all of the contemporary Dominican cigarettes and everything else he had in there and replaced them with cigarettes and gum that had the proper wrappings of the Cuban brands from the 1950's. I had the wrappers manufactured while still in Los Angeles. For an extra touch, we added a small candle and a little picture of Jesus. An awesome looking prop if I do say so myself.

Well, Sydney had a technical adviser for most of the shoot to be certain everything on set looked authentic. The adviser was a well-respected Cuban director named Teton. I made my way up to Syd, thinking he not only was going to thank me for the awesome three days of work but also wanted to tell me how cool the cigarette box looked. I was standing there in front of him waiting for my well deserved pat on the head, when he turned to me and shouted, "Get those fucking Galois cigarettes out of there! Don't you do your research?"

What had apparently happened was that just as they were about to roll, Teton pointed out to Sydney that he didn't recall ever seeing Galois cigarettes in Cuba. In fact, although the Galois label had not changed in all of those years, it was possible that he was right and they never did exist in Cuba. I did however have about eight other brands of cigarettes in that box that were more visible and were absolutely in Cuba during that time period. To be honest, I may in fact have been mistaken and should not have put Galois in the box. All that work shot straight to hell over a pack of cigarettes.

More *Havana*

Now the tone was clearly set and I knew what I had in store for me for the remainder of the show. We did, however, come up with a new term that brought us all a chuckle: "Pollacking"—or "getting Pollacked." Those were the new terms for getting reamed by Syd. The camera crew was immune to Pollacking because they were teacher's pets. The grips and electricians were exempt because they worked for the camera department. The script supervisor was a close friend of Syd's, so she was safe. The sound department had a free pass as they had done *Out of Africa* with him. That left the following departments ripe and easy pickings for getting Pollacked: the assistant directors, hair, wardrobe, and us. The makeup department was fine because Redford's long-time makeup man was running it. The rest of us were sitting ducks for Sydney's wrath.

Syd frequently Pollacked the hair department. The head of that department was the producer's wife, but Sydney had not wanted her in the first place, so she took her share of Pollackings. The on-set wardrobe people would occasionally get a good Pollacking, and you already know what my team was experiencing.

To add insult to injury, I had a real wake-up call during this unpleasant time period. I received word from Ron Howard's people that he wanted me to do *Backdraft*, which was to be shot totally on location in Chicago. I accepted the job, as it would begin pre-production shortly after the conclusion of my time in Santo Domingo. I called home to inform my family. When my son got on the phone, I told him about the job in Chicago. He then asked, "Dad, how long will you be home from the Dominican Republic before you have to leave for Chicago?"

I said, "About three weeks, son."

He then hit me with, "Well, Dad, do you think you can practice soccer with me every day because the kids are picking me last, and it makes me feel bad."

Derek is thirty-two years old now, but it still makes me sad when I think about that conversation. I said, "Derek, I changed my mind, and I'm not going to Chicago. I will practice with you every day for as long as you want."

"Thanks Daddy. I love you."

"I love you too, Son."

After a couple of phone calls I was able to reach Ron personally at his home. I told him about the conversation I'd had with my son. I explained that I was sorry that I had accepted the job and now was going to back out, but needed to go home and be with my children. Ron responded exactly as I imagined he would. To this day I clearly remember what he said, "I'm sorry you won't be able to be with us, but it takes courage to know when to put on the brakes." He told me that he supported my decision and that I need not feel badly about it. That is the type of human being Ron Howard is.

* * *

The daily grind of working on *Havana* and the pressure of dodging verbal abuse were difficult tasks. When Jimmy and I would meet in the morning to hop on the crew bus, we would literally ask God to help us get through the day. Every day was a test of enduring the grueling heat and the sour moods of our leader, who had discovered there was not much chemistry between his two leading actors.

Several weeks into shooting, we embarked on another three-night sequence involving Redford, Lena Olin, and a Greek actor by the name of Jorgo Voyagis, who played Olin's husband. The scene took place in a restaurant. Food sequences tend to be difficult for several reasons. First of all, most actors hate to eat on film because they don't want to talk with food in their mouths. Also, depending on what they are eating, issues will be raised: Is it warm and tasty enough for them to enjoy? Does the food on the plate need replenishing between takes? Did the actors take a drink of their beverages, which would then need refilling? Close attention must be paid to these things. Keep in mind that more often than not, adjustments need to be made between takes. Props need to be reset, actors may need a small makeup or hair touch up, or the soundman may need to adjust a hidden microphone. There are several reasons why when we hear "Cut!" we are ready to jump in and make the necessary adjustments as quickly as possible to avoid time delays.

Directors, of course, realize this. However, Sydney found it annoying when these adjustments took place. He would yell with increasing volume, "Guys, guys, JESUS, GUYS! It's like a wrecking crew running in every time I yell cut!" It felt as if we were just necessary evils for him to endure.

We filmed in the restaurant for three nights. In the middle of this restaurant, the set decorator had dressed in an entire pig on a platter with an apple stuffed in its mouth and parsley up its ass. I hated this thing. It was disgusting. What made matters worse was that he never replaced the pig with a fresh one so by night number three, this pig was really getting ripe. The crew was beginning to complain about the stench. Mitch, one of our grips yelled out, "It sure would be a feather in our cap if we could get one more night out of this pig!" We all got a laugh out of that one, but it didn't stop the odor. Jimmy—God bless the guy—picked up the platter the pig was on and, gagging, took it off the set and sprayed the shit out of it with Lysol. As I recall, that got the pig and the crew through the evening, ending the three nights of hell.

That might just have been about the only hardy laugh I had my entire time over there. Well... there was one other hilarious moment; not long after lunch one day during prep, Jimmy felt something "coming on". For some reason the warehouse door was locked, so he had to run to a nearby porta-potty. After about 10 minutes, an agitated Jimmy comes storming out shouting, "BEAN SKINS! BEAN SKINS! That's all that ever comes out of me here! BEAN SKINS!" Oh man, I couldn't catch my breath!

A few days after we shot the restaurant sequence, the rumors were flying that Sydney was not happy with Jorgo's performance. Sure enough, word came down that the entire sequence was to be re-shot at a later time with Raul Julia replacing Jorgo.

When I heard about this, I wanted to go up to Syd and say, "What the fuck is wrong with you? Don't you audition your actors properly?"

Several years later I was having a drink in a bar. I picked up a cocktail napkin when I noticed there was a trivia question printed on it: What was the biggest box office flop of 1991? I turned the napkin over... yep, that's right... *Havana*.

I smiled, raised my glass and said, *"Here's to ya, Syd!"*

Allan Levine
(June 27, 1928–September 28, 1999)
This is my father, the man who made it all possible!

CBS Radford Studio City, California, 1973
Yours truly at the time of my very first day in the
Motion Picture Industry.

1976 *The Last Tycoon*
David and I made our escape from this door and
stairway at Paramount Studios after being scolded by
Elia Kazan in February 1976.

1976 *The Last Tycoon*
Robert Mitchum's dressing room.
When Robert Mitchum opened his dressing room door, we
were all hit by a wall of marijuana smoke.

1980 *Hard Country*
Tanya Tucker and I are on the set of *Hard Country* starring
Jan-Michael Vincent and Kim Basinger.
Los Angeles, California

1984 *Cocoon*
Ron Howard was a pleasure to work with.
St. Petersburg, Florida

1984 *Cocoon*
Richard Zanuck and Ron Howard going
over something important!
St. Petersburg, Florida

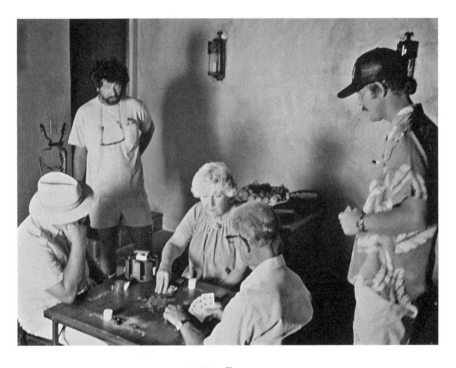

1984 *Cocoon*
I am paying close attention onset as Ron Howard
directs our heroes, Wilford Brimley, Maureen Stapleton,
and Hume Cronyn.
St. Petersburg, Florida

1984 *Cocoon*
Here I am between two aliens,
Tyrone Power Jr. (left) and Mike Nomad (right).
St. Petersburg, Florida

1984 *Cocoon*
Wilford Brimley, Don Ameche, and me
Camaraderie off the set in St. Petersburg, Florida

Close-up of Cocoons

1984 *Cocoon*
Top photo: Watching the Cocoons gaining strength and
energy at the bottom of the pool.
Bottom photo: Ron Howard lining up a shot.
St. Petersburg, Florida

Harvey Hubert
The man who built the box that caught fire!
St. Petersburg, Florida

1984 *Cocoon*
This is me chillin' in the very unchilled pool house location
in St. Petersburg, Florida.

1984 *Cocoon*

Here I am on my "badass" daily transportation from the
apartment I shared with my family to the crew bus in
St. Petersburg, Florida.

1987 *Cocoon*
Not to be outdone by the grips' bar, CLUB DUZ (open 24 hours), the prop department opened a bigger better bar, PUB LEVINE (open 25 hours a day–8 days a week), on our truck. Bottom right, "Cheers" from Jimmy "Bean Skins" Robinson. Miami, Florida

1985 *Pee-wee's Big Adventure*
Pee-wee Herman loves his bike, but it gets stolen. When he
shows these photos of his bike to a fraudulent psychic named
Madame Ruby, she tells him that the bike is hidden in the
basement of the Alamo Mission in San Antonio.
And the adventure begins...

My son Derek Levine and me
The bust statue between us is my father, Allan Levine,
Founder of the Hand Prop Room, Inc. (1974), a 30,000-square
foot warehouse with over a million props (www.hpr.com).
Derek is now manager of the prop returns department.
5700 Venice Blvd, Los Angeles, California

"A picture is worth a thousand words."
Stephen Gibson, Prop Man

A well-stocked 48-foot prop truck

Organization is of the utmost importance to a prop crew. As you can see by the one pictured here, these trucks are not designed to be loaded and unloaded. Currently, a 20th Century Fox executive has ruled that prop masters may not use their own trucks, but they must download their equipment into an empty truck about half the size as a money-saving measure. Taking away a well-outfitted trailer is like taking the scalpel from the surgeon while expecting the same end result.

August 10, 1994

Dear Ron Howard Sir,

Hi. I'm Danielle Levine. If it would be okay, do you think my father (Steve Levine) must be on the ~~scene~~ when they're in the Commander Module, and it's 25 degres, do you think he can just stay outside? You can reach me at: (310)   or (310)

Thanks for your time!

Miss Danielle Jessica Levine

1995 *Apollo 13*
Here I am with "Bean Skins" Jimmy Robinson on the
refrigerated set of *Apollo 13*. This cold set was created so that
we could see the actors' breath in the disabled LEM Module.
Universal Studios, Los Angeles, California

Dear Steve, Jimmy & Terri,

What a pleasant surprise to receive the ring Kathleen wore in the movie. It was very thoughtful of you to think of me and I will treasure it forever.

From the beginnings of the book and now the movie all the fears tears and elation of the events of 25 years ago have resurfaced and I am still moved by all of it —

Please excuse me for being so late in thanking you — I haven't been in our Texas home so I wasn't aware the package was waiting for me until last week when Jim arrived there.

Looking forward to June and the release of Apollo XIII

In deep appreciation
Marilyn Lovell

March Third

RON HOWARD
Co-CEO

May 1, 1995

Mr. Steve Levine
1334 12th Street #A
Manhatten Beach, CA 90266

Dear Steve,

    It is hard for me to fathom but I realized that there is
a discernible light at the end of the APOLLO 13 tunnel. We
have a final screening (barring some new idea I want to
terrorize everyone with by trying out, of course) tomorrow
night. Our early exposure to the media has indicated great
support and enthusiasm. I know that of all the projects,
this one has been the most challenging, and in many ways, the
most gratifying. The Digital Domain work is looking strong
and of course the performances, led by Tom, are a huge asset.

    Ed Gibson (a Skylab astronaut) who helped us out on the
"white room" days commented to me the other day that he was
unprepared for the display of unified effort and achievement
that he witnessed while he was with us. I, of course, told
him that even this crew could have a couple of lucky days,
but seriously, I think that most of the NASA veterans were
pleased, make that, relieved, by the degree of care and
attention to detail that we were maintaining. I know I am
very proud of the extra push everyone gave.

    Audiences are really responding well to the movie in our
preview screenings, and they, too, seem to appreciate the
authenticity and realism along with the story and the actors.
The test scores have been, well... I don't like to put too
much stock in those but... awfully damned exciting, and if
they translate to box-office, Universal should be very happy
(whoever they turn out to be on June 30th). Sid Sheinberg,
Tom Pollock, Casey Silver and the entire Universal marketing
group in fact seems to be ecstatic about the movie, which
sure beats the hell out of a poke in the eye with a sharp
stick. I know this, because shortly after listening to their
glowing remarks, I actually poked myself in the eye with a
sharp stick, and I like the compliments a whole lot better.

Continued...

IMAGINE ENTERTAINMENT
1925 Century Park East
Twenty-third Floor
Los Angeles, CA 90067
Tel 310.277.1665
Fax 310.785.0107

The NASA people continue to simply communicate their
thanks for making the movie with this degree of integrity,
because they feel that it could have positive long term
effects on the space program. Wouldn't that be great? I
just hope they like it well enough to go see it a second time
and bring along a friend!

You really did a terrific job, on APOLLO 13, Steve. The
overall attention to detail and the basic grunt work all paid
off in deal dividends for the movie. On a show where
research and thoroughness was crucial, you and your team were
really leading the charge. I appreciate it, and hope you
like the movie when you see it.

Regards,

Ron Howard

1983 *All of Me*
During a day of shooting in downtown Los Angeles,
Steve Martin, Carl Reiner, and I are in deep contemplation.

1983 *All of Me*
In this photo, Lily Tomlin is holding the doll that I had
made for her, to her specific specifications.
Los Angeles, California

1985 "Gung Ho" (starring Michael Keaton)
Ron Howard, Louisa Velis (Ron's very long-time assistant),
and I are in the Pittsburgh Pirate dugout at
the Old Three Rivers Stadium.
Pittsburgh, Pennsylvania

8.3.93

Steve!

It's been so
great our 2ⁿᵈ
picture together.
Besides your
wonderful
work, it's
like having a
friend and
family with
me. Thank you,

Luis

This is a thank you note from the fine director,
Luis Mandoki, who I worked for on *Born Yesterday* and
When A Man Loves A Woman.

CHAPTER 15

Director's Chairs

Probably around the time talkies became popular, the director's chair became the prop master's responsibility. This has been an ever-increasing pain in the ass for several reasons.

First of all the term, "director's chair" is misleading right off the bat. A director's chair would indicate just that, a chair for the director. However, it is not just a chair for the director. It is also a chair for the script supervisor, the numerous and ever-growing list of producers, the writers, the regular cast members, and guest cast. For an idea of how many that might be, tune in to any of the weekly episodes of a one-hour action, medical, police, or detective show and check out the amount of folks who receive screen credits at the beginning of the episode. That's where the count begins. In addition, we must carry extra chairs for the guests of the producers and for behind-the-scene interviews that are conducted away from set by the likes of *Entertainment Tonight* or any of the companies that interview the stars. We also carry chairs for network executives, or "The Suits". I can understand the need for director's chairs. The hours are long; the wait time for lighting and the setting up of shots all take time.

If you are not familiar with what director's chairs are, they are wood-framed chairs with canvas seats and backs that are designed to be folded and moved. The problem is, the last thing any prop department wants to do is hold up filming for any reason. Budgets are controlled by an ever-increasing tight fistedness and the chairs take precious time away from the tasks at hand.

It's very time consuming at the end of a scene to fold and move several chairs and then re-set them for the next scene. Keep in mind that at the same time we are dealing with the chairs, we need to collect the props from the previous scene and get the props ready for the next one. Also, the people sitting in these chairs tend to leave heavy coats, shoulder bags, laptops, food, books, and any number of things that need to be removed before the chairs can be folded and moved. They put empty coffee cups, gum wrappers, and things that should be thrown into a trash can into the chair's side-pockets. Since it's become very difficult these days to get extra help, you can see how the chairs have become a real issue to contend with.

When I started in the industry, the director would sit directly next to the camera to watch the actors perform the scene. In some films from the 40's and 50's, you may even be able to see the director's cigarette smoke wafting into the shot. In those days at the conclusion of the scene, if the director was happy, he would then have to ask the camera operator how it looked through the lens. Not so today. Video playback is on virtually every set and with it came what is known as "video village."

Video village is an area off of the set where the director and his group watch the scene unfold on video monitors. In many cases, particularly pilots (the first episode that introduces a new show), there can be two video villages, which makes for even more chairs as the studio executives like to monitor the activities. Most of us prop people would prefer that either the production assistants or the craft service department take the chair duty.

The role of the craft service person has evolved greatly over the years. Up until the early 80's or thereabouts, their job was to help any department that needed temporary assistance. For example, if an extra boom mike would help the sound department, the craft service person may hold a boom pole. If the grips needed a hand lifting a dolly up a flight of stairs, he would help with that, hence the name, craft service. This is no longer the case. Today craft service people are in charge of onset food, coffee, and snacks, which has become a full-time job. They are not expected to jump in and help the crafts anymore. It is nice to have food available. A hungry crew is a cranky crew; however, it leaves a hole that the old-school craft service person once filled.

It is important to note that some prop people will certainly disagree with me in terms of the chairs, and I respect their point of view. Their take is simply this: the more our union gives away, the easier it is for producers to slowly remove more of our responsibilities, eventually eliminating our position totally. As difficult as this is for me to grasp, it is true that many executives, particularly the ones that don't understand what our jobs are, will stop at nothing to find new ways to save money. I think what they would like to do would be to further blur the lines for each department. The goal would be to add work to each craft while eliminating key positions, thus saving money.

As I write this, 20th Century Fox has an executive (you know who you are) that not only has begun to eliminate the on-set dresser job, but has now banned the key grips, the gaffers (head lighting technicians), and property masters from using their own personal 40- to 48-foot work trailers that have taken them years to outfit for their specific needs. In their place they are issued substantially smaller, empty work trailers and are instructed to cram what they need into them.

By doing this, the rental for the trailer to the department head is eliminated. Taking away a well-outfitted trailer is like taking the scalpel from the surgeon while expecting the same end result. While I am sure the brainchild that came up with this idea is sitting in his nice comfy office collecting his share of money and pats on the back, he should be aware of countless crew members busting their butts trying to do the best job they can while being put at a tremendous disadvantage. I know because the last show I did at Fox was without our prop truck. He is not a well-liked person down here in the trenches.

CHAPTER 16

Rush

Having worked for Richard and Lili Zanuck on both *Cocoon* films, I was their choice to be the property master on Lili's directorial debut, *Rush*. The film is based on the book written by Kim Wozencraft. Kim and her male partner were narcotics agents in the '70's in Texas. In the line of duty, they developed a drug habit themselves. Drug dealers don't trust new buyers unless they are willing to use the drug in their presence. Jennifer Jason Leigh and Jason Patric were the lead characters and delivered outstanding performances portraying a veteran narc and his new female partner, both of whom were willing to do whatever the job required to make the bust.

I think the film is worth seeing; and if you choose to see it, pay close attention to the props, particularly the drugs and drug paraphernalia, as they were of utmost importance for the film's credibility. My good friend and assistant "Bean Skins" Jimmy and I researched them in great detail.

There are some memorable scenes that deserve to be singled out, especially now that I am going to give you some background on them. First, let's look at the opening shot of the film. I must first preface this by admitting that I am today, and have been for forty years, a huge fan of the Allman Brothers Band. To my delight, Gregg Allman was cast as *Will Gaines,* the town's biggest drug dealer and badass dude. I have never been star-struck by actors, as I have been around or worked with them for most of my life, but I do get star-struck when I see rock stars as I have not had many occasions to see or work with them. Gregg, in my opinion, is one of the greatest blues vocalists of all time, and his band is in the Rock and Roll Hall of Fame.

An extremely difficult and very impressive shot kicks off this film. From the beginning of the scene, which starts with the sound of the tumblers in a safe's spinning knob, until the end of the scene where the audience sees an aerial view of the tail lights on Gregg's car driving down the road and exiting the frame, there is no cut in the film. It is one continuous shot, and I'm going to describe how it was achieved.

The first thing the audience sees is a black screen but hears what will soon be discovered as the sound of the safe's tumblers. As the picture comes into view we see a wall safe being opened, revealing Gregg removing a gun and a wad of cash. Grabbing these items, he then walks over to his desk. To accomplish this, the safe was built into a collapsible wall, which was open at the back. That is where the camera lens was placed. As Gregg opens the safe door his face is revealed, as is the gun and the money. The wall is then pushed aside allowing the cameraman to follow him to his desk. As Gregg turns to walk out of the room, the cameraman maneuvers behind him and follows him down a flight of stairs and into the bar where he walks over to confer with a band member.

At this point, the cameraman takes the camera off of Gregg for a moment, pans around the bar, and stops on a shot of Jason Patric's character shooting pool with a beautiful young woman. (That woman was the real Mrs. Allman at the time.) The camera then pans back around to focus on Gregg, as it follows him making his way through the crowd, exiting the bar via swinging saloon doors, walking outside, and getting into his car. The cameraman then steps onto a floorboard of what is known as a Chapman crane, which slowly rises to about fifty feet, providing the audience with an aerial view of Gregg's car pulling out of the parking lot and driving down the road until the taillights fade from view. It's one of my favorite opening shots of all time.

To accomplish what I just described, there is a time-consuming and intricate set-up process that is very carefully choreographed. This type of shot is known as a Steadicam shot. A Steadicam is a stabilizing mount for a handheld motion picture camera, which mechanically isolates the operator's movement from the camera, allowing a very smooth shot even when the operator is moving quickly over an uneven surface. The combination of the mount and the camera are commonly referred to as a Steadicam.

Another extraordinary scene runs for about eight of the most engaging minutes I have ever seen on film. A character is introduced as *Willie Red* and the actor portraying him is a fellow by the name of Special K. McCray. *Willie Red* is a hardcore drug dealer, and Special really nails it. Lili said this was the hardest role of the film to cast. Many auditioned to no avail. Special K. heard about the part and sent Lili a homemade video audition. She liked it enough to fly him out to audition in person. The guy landed the part right then and there, and you will see why if you watch the film. I truly enjoyed being on set and watching him work. He even came up with some of his own dialogue himself (which is rarely accepted by writers and directors); and it was so perfect for the character that Special was given all the freedom he needed. I won't even try to describe this scene or his performance because it wouldn't do justice to either. This is a scene that one must experience first-hand to understand what I'm talking about.

During the course of shooting, I flew home for a long weekend to see my wife and kids. The night I flew back to

Texas, I was waiting to board my flight when a guy acting rather strangely caught my eye. He was pacing back and forth and seemed to be muttering to himself. I observed him for a while and even contemplated alerting security. When it was time to board, although feeling uncomfortable about this guy, I went ahead and boarded also. We had an uneventful flight to Houston and by the time we landed, I had totally forgotten about this strange fellow.

Two or three days later we were scheduled to shoot a scene with Jennifer's character making a drug buy. In this scenario, she was purchasing a load of downers known as "blue ringers". My assistant and I were setting up the director's chairs, having all the necessary props with us on set and were getting ready for rehearsal. The assistant director called the actors to set. Who do you think shows up playing the drug dealer? None other than the weirdo from the flight! Not a weirdo at all, but a fine actor by the name of William Sadler. What he was doing at the airport was going over his lines to himself. Later, I told him that I had seen him prior to our flight and what I had thought. We had a good laugh about the whole thing.

This scene begins with Jennifer entering the Sadler character's residence to the sounds of Jimi Hendrix blaring in the background. Sadler plays the part of a bizarre and creepy drug dealer who, among other drugs, sells the blue ringers. Although I found suitable substitutes for other pills, I couldn't find anything to replicate this particular pill that got its name due to a distinct blue line that looks like a thin ring around the capsule. We had to fabricate them by purchasing empty gel capsules and filling them with the substance that drug dealers use to cut their cocaine, which can be purchased in head shops. Then we purchased very thin blue tape and wrapped each of the filled gel caps individually. We needed at least enough pills to fill a common sized cigar box. This was very time consuming, so when we went to Galveston to shoot a sequence featuring Jennifer running on the beach, we left our local hire from Houston to handle this tedious task.

I had to simulate many different types of drugs for the film. I found a great source for pills in a magazine. *High Times* is a magazine that sells pills made up of legal substances that appear to be the real thing. For the marijuana, we used catnip and for the buds, we used portions of plants that looked like marijuana plant tops, sprayed them with adhesive glue and rolled them in the catnip. If a joint needed to be smoked, we rolled it with herbal cigarette ingredients. But what about heroin? I had never seen heroin before. I knew a recovering addict here in L.A. who not only made up simulated substances for me but also worked with the actors to familiarize them with methods of cooking and shooting the drug. I learned the method as well. It is imperative to know how props work as well as supplying them. In Texas, we had a technical adviser on set with us whenever there was simulated drug use. He had been clean for twenty years and ran a rehab program.

There is one particular scene in the film that has Jason showing Jennifer how to inject the stuff. The most common way to simulate this is to use what is known as a retractable needle. The needle is attached to a spring and as the actor puts pressure on it, the needle goes into the body of the syringe giving the illusion that it is penetrating the arm or wherever the injection occurs. However, in this case, Jason came up with something that I had never heard of before. He wanted to actually inject himself with a saline solution. That is exactly what he did, but unfortunately with the way the film was cut, the audience doesn't see how real it was because the needle wasn't shown exiting his arm. We had both a doctor and a technical advisor on set for this.

Sam Elliot plays the lead detective in charge of this particular case. As you know, Sam is an actor with a macho presence and frequently plays tough-guy cowboy roles with that big droopy mustache and deep voice. I had worked with him many years prior to this on a movie made for television. He chewed Copenhagen at that time, and one afternoon on set, reached into his back pocket and pulled out a can of his "dip". Taking a large pinch he offered me some too. Here was this big macho dude offering the stuff to me, and I didn't want to seem like a pussy so I reached in, took a "big ol' pinch'" and shoved it down between my lower lip and gums as I had seen it done before, and pretended like I knew what I was doing. We stood on the stage talking for a few minutes until I started feeling the effect of this shit. I politely excused myself as inconspicuously as possible, as to not tip off the fact that I was rapidly disintegrating. I spit it out as soon as I was out of sight and immediately had to lie down. I was nauseated, and my head was pounding. I notified my assistant of the situation, found an isolated spot on stage, and plopped down on the ground. Apparently even if you are a chewer or dipper or whatever you call it, Copenhagen is for the advanced user. It's like a kid trying to smoke for the first time and inhaling a camel non-filter. I have never dipped again.

As we were approaching the end of our shoot in Texas, the Zanucks asked me to do their next film, *Rich in Love*, to be shot in South Carolina. I had already been away from home for three months. The kids had visited me for about two weeks while I was in Houston, but other than a quick weekend in Los Angeles I hadn't seen them. As much as I regretted turning the show down, I really wanted to be with my kids. Turning down the opportunity to work with people like the Zanucks and Ron Howard is very difficult because they understand and appreciate our contribution to their projects and they treat their crews very well. Not accepting the job also increases the risk of losing your place as their first choice because they might find another person who also does a great job, and that person will be fresher in their minds for their next project.

CHAPTER 17

Born Yesterday

I had been working on a Steven Bochco television series called *Civil Wars*, starring Mariel Hemingway, about the trials and tribulations of a group of lawyers. Just as the first season was ending, I took a feature film entitled *Born Yesterday*, starring Don Johnson and Melanie Griffith. The other lead went to John Goodman, which delayed our first day of shooting for six weeks due to John being committed to another project. The good news was that I received an additional six weeks of prep time for *Born Yesterday*. The bad news was that by the time I finished that film, it was too late for me to return for the second season of *Civil Wars*.

We shot *Born Yesterday* mostly in Los Angeles, but we also worked in Washington D.C. for a week or two. During my preparation period, I had no access to the lead actors due to their scheduling issues. This presented a few problems early on, as a couple of the props the director and I had thought would work for Melanie and Don had to be changed in a bit of a rush, but nothing that caused any delays or real headaches.

One thing that did happen centered on a pair of sunglasses Melanie was to wear on camera. As you have learned, glasses are considered props, not wardrobe. Since I had no chance to meet with Melanie prior to shooting, I obtained several pairs of sunglasses in hopes she would find a pair that would suit her.

On the first day of shooting I showed her the options. She didn't want any of them, preferring instead to wear her own personal pair, which she then handed to me. Whenever a principal actor wears glasses, it is imperative to have them doubled, in case the first pair is either lost or broken. I told her I would like to hold on to her glasses to aid me in finding a matching pair. She informed me that she would like her glasses returned to her as soon as possible. I then asked if she remembered where her glasses had been purchased. "Somewhere in France," was her reply. *Wow, thanks for the help!*

This was before the Internet, and I only had one assistant, so it was a real challenge to figure out the logistics of how to make this happen quickly. Melanie didn't wear them on camera for the first few weeks because we were filming indoors, so I thought I had a little time. I had a few ideas about how I could accomplish this, but it wasn't first on my priority list as I had other more pressing issues.

Two days later, a production assistant informed me that Melanie would like to see me at her motor home. *Uh-oh.* I knocked on her door. A second later she answered and asked, "Have you gotten a double for my sunglasses yet?"

"No, not quite yet," I said.

"Well, why not?"

"Gee Melanie, I've been pretty busy, but I will have them soon".

After that little exchange, I figured I'd better get on this quickly. I certainly didn't need the lead actress being unhappy with me the first week of shooting with ten weeks left to go.

Within a few days, I found a pair that wasn't exact, but close enough to use as a backup and was able to return her sunglasses to her. The reason I tell this story is to illustrate how unrealistic some stars can become (certainly not just

Melanie). During the course of filming, lead actors and actresses have people scrambling to fulfill their every wish.

Here are a few general examples: The star arrives to work and requests a Starbucks non-fat, half-caf-mochachino-espresso combo with two and a half squirts of hazelnut syrup and a dash of vanilla nut. A driver will immediately be sent to fulfill this wish.

Their motor home is equipped with a teakettle and selection of tea. The star, however, has just seen a really cool, new way to brew tea. The expensive brewing appliance is sold at The Beverly Center (an exclusive mall in West Hollywood). The star tells the production assistant, who immediately radios the transportation department. Once again, a driver is on his way.

Maybe the star feels a little run down. Not to worry; the doctor will be there shortly with a vitamin B-12 shot. When a request is made and people jump, stars become conditioned to expect immediate results.

I don't want to give Melanie a bad rap because other than the incident with the sunglasses, she was fine. These are simply examples to illustrate how many A-list actors are treated.

As far as Don Johnson was concerned, I had heard he could be a bit on the demanding side. He actually treated me quite well, and I never had the slightest bit of trouble with him. I noticed early on that he liked to sit close to the playback monitor to check out his performance after takes. I also noticed that at other times he preferred to distance himself from the group while sitting on stage. I decided to get him two director's chairs with his name on both, keeping one at the monitor and one a distance away. He loved this idea. It immediately put me in his good graces. I would also go into his motor home in the morning before he arrived and neatly lay out his personal props: eyeglasses, leather notepad, gold plated pen, his pocket watch, and a pack of Marlboro mediums. One day he told me he thought I was the best prop man he had ever worked with. I have a feeling this had more to do with the two chairs and personal prop set-up than anything else, but I happily accepted the compliment. We actually had an opportunity to have some pretty good talks during the course of the show, and I really liked Don.

CHAPTER 18

Divorce as a Wake-Up Call

Shortly after wrapping *Born Yesterday* in 1992, I was blind-sided by my wife wanting a divorce. This hit me hard and really pulled the rug from under my feet, as facing life without living in the same house as my wife and children devastated me. We had been together since the age of twenty-three, and here I was, forty-one years old and not prepared in any way for being without her. It was clear that I had no choice in the matter; she wanted to move on with her life. The truth be told, I certainly had my part in the dissolution. The business often took me away to distant locations far from my home and family for months at a time; and even when I was working in town, the hours were extremely grueling and long. More importantly, I wasn't evolving in my personal life. She, on the other hand was, and was becoming more of a spiritual woman. At that time in my life, I didn't even know what that meant.

My children were really lifesavers for me at that time. I rented an apartment two miles from where they were living and took them with me every weekend. If I could get away from the set, I would pick them up during the week as well. Luckily, my ex was very cooperative when it came to my spending time with the kids. Now that I'm a grandfather and spend time with my granddaughter, I realize that I missed out on many of the beautiful milestones that are so precious in a child's formative years: the first bath, rolling over, sitting up, the first giggle. Nothing can be done about that now other than me continuing to try to be the best, present, loving father and grandfather that I can be.

In the midst of what was a devastating time for me, I still had to work. The next two films I worked on were *When A Man Loves A Woman* starring Meg Ryan and Andy Garcia and a John Singleton film entitled *Higher Learning*.

Being In the frame of mind that I was in, I don't recall much about those experiences other than them being the same daily grind to which I had become accustomed.

CHAPTER 19

Apollo 13

I am very proud of my resume as it reflects years of hard work, but I'm probably most proud of my work on *Apollo 13*. As I was wrapping up *Higher Learning*, I received a call from a producer asking me to do Ron Howard's upcoming film. I hadn't seen Ron in ten years; the last film with him being *Gung Ho*. I was very flattered that after all that time, he would still remember me and offer me this job.

I knew absolutely nothing about the space program and really never had much interest in it up until that point. I certainly had my work cut out for me, as I knew that there was a tremendous amount of research to be done. Universal and Imagine (Ron and Brian Grazer's company) were very fair about giving me the preparation time necessary for a project of this magnitude. Early on, I flew to NASA in Houston, where I spent several days asking questions and observing the different departments. This is where mission control is located. I already had several photos and text research on this particular mission, but of course going there and seeing it in person was of tremendous value.

I had a liaison who got me started, and over the course of several days, I asked a great deal of questions to the folks, some of whom had actually been there during the time of that particular flight. Everyone was accommodating and happy to answer all of my questions, as they were excited that this film about this mission was going into production. I left there with an abundance of detailed information that I needed for this project, but also an education for myself as well as an appreciation for the space program and everyone involved. The teamwork that it takes, including those that build the vessels, to mission control, to the astronauts, has to be flawless for a mission's success.

After NASA, I flew to Kansas Cosmosphere in Hutchinson, Kansas. They build replica spacecraft for many museums, including the Smithsonian, and had already been contracted to build the Apollo capsules for our film. They also have their own museum and run a wonderful space camp for kids. My job would have been so much more difficult had it not been for the people at this unbelievable space center. Like my time in Houston, I spent a few days there learning and researching—and I think I can say for the first time, *truly* comprehended how incredible it was that in 1969 we had men walking on the moon!

I went over my entire prop breakdown with them focusing on every detail that had anything to do with the spacecraft. They were able to supply me with several props including the pieces of the carbon monoxide filter that were scattered on a table in one memorable scene. The scene depicts how the astronauts had to construct a square box to fit into a round hole in order to keep them from dying of carbon monoxide poisoning. To this day, anytime I'm in a conversation with someone who finds out that I did the props for *Apollo 13*, that's almost always the first scene that they want to talk about. They are curious and have so many questions as to how I was able to duplicate these items. In the spirit of "giving props where props are due," I tell them it was with the help of the brilliant staff at Kansas Cosmosphere.

I continued my contact with the folks at the space center throughout the entire shooting process. Several of their representatives spent time on set with us in Los Angeles at Universal Studios.

While doing my research at Kansas Cosmosphere, I had the opportunity to sit in an exact replica of the Gemini VII capsule that Jim Lovell (The Apollo 13 captain) and Frank Borman had circled the earth for fourteen days in December 1965. I was surprised that it was so small and cramped, and amazed that anyone could handle being inside of that thing, especially for that amount of time.

When I returned to L.A., I had the privilege and honor of being able to sit down with Mr. Lovell and go over the details of the mission with him. By now I had more knowledge about the mission so my questions for him were much more specific than those I had when I was in Houston and Kansas.

Prior to our meeting, I was anticipating a staunch military man, strictly business, with little or no sense of humor. This assumption couldn't have been further from the truth. He was very engaging, friendly, and happy to answer all of my questions. What struck me most was his keen sense of humor. Toward the end of our talk, I told him about my experience sitting inside the Gemini VII replica. I *had* to ask him how he could possibly handle being confined in such a small craft for that amount of time. He laughed and jokingly said, "*That* wasn't the hard part; the hard part was sitting next to Borman for so long!" Lovell would not be with us for the shooting of the film, as he was scheduled to be on a book tour for *Apollo 13: Lost Moon*, the book from which the film was based.

The production designer on *Apollo 13* was a fellow we will refer to as Michael. For reasons I never understood, he didn't like me. He went to Ron and our first assistant director during the preparation period and told them he didn't have confidence in me. They responded by telling him not to worry because they had both worked with me in the past and knew quite well that I was very capable of doing my job. I know this conversation did indeed take place because the assistant director told me about it over lunch one day. I found the whole thing a bit strange since other than Sydney Pollack, I had never had my abilities questioned, especially *after* I was already hired.

But to be honest, I found him to be a very peculiar fellow. Our relationship on the film was certainly not great but not bad either. It was one of simply tolerating one another. I actually went out of my way to break the ice and try to warm up to the guy but was unsuccessful.

Here's the irony of this business: Michael received an Academy Award nomination for Production Design (the overall look of a film). Remember in an earlier chapter I explained how the prop department falls under the art department? Well, during the three months of shooting, I received several compliments for my team's hard work, including the best one from Dave Scott. Dave was our on-set technical adviser in Lovell's absence and a former astronaut himself. He was impressed that I was able to duplicate my props as well as I did, paying close attention to detail, and he was particularly amazed that I had re-created the flight manuals to look exactly as he had remembered them to look. He expressed that to me as we talked one night outside the stage. When he went back inside, I looked up at the moon and thought, *Holy shit, I just spent time talking to a guy who actually walked around up there!* In addition, he was the first man to drive a lunar rover on the moon and the seventh man to walk on it as the captain of Apollo 15. Pretty damn good qualifications for judging the authenticity of my work, wouldn't you say? Well... as I said, Michael was nominated for an Academy Award for "his" work and never once thanked me for my contribution or uttered a kind word. So Michael, if you happen to be reading my book, "You're welcome... and go FUCK YOURSELF!"

* * *

If you saw the film, perhaps you remember the scene outside the Lovell home where the press begins arriving with its equipment to cover the story of the now endangered flight. In real life and the film, at this stage of the mission, most of America was following this event, as was much of the world. As there were many extras involved in this scene (and you now know what that entails), my team and I were quite busy. In the midst of this, Todd, one of Ron's producers walked over to me and asked me to take care of his dog for a few minutes. He handed me the leash and walked away. This was a bulldog like the one from *Jake and the Fatman,* for those of you who can remember that far back. I was now stuck with this dog that proceeded to immediately walk over to a stack of sandbags that belonged to the grips, crank up his leg, and pee all over them. I found this to be quite funny; however, I'm sure the grips wouldn't have.

Written into the script is a scene where *Marilyn Lovell* is taking a shower. The lovely Kathleen Quinlan played *Marilyn*. While in the shower, her wedding ring slips off of her finger and goes down the drain. This is an incident that actually did happen to *Marilyn*. There are occasions when a story is being written, that is based on real-life events, where the writers exercise what is known as "creative license" to enhance the drama of a film; they stay true to the core of the event but may alter or embellish the details surrounding it. That was not the case with this incident.

We found out exactly what type of ring she had been wearing and duplicated it; making one that was more expensive for Kathleen to wear in the film, and several other less expensive ones to go down the drain. When the film completed photography, I mailed Marilyn the ring that Kathleen had worn so she could have a reasonable facsimile of her actual ring that slid down the drain so many years ago. I still have the lovely thank-you note that Mrs. Lovell sent to me, which I've included in the photographs in this book.

I want to quickly point out an important continuity issue; when a prop such as a ring goes down the drain, it is important to note what scene number in which that happens, so we don't accidently give the actress the ring to wear in a scene that appears in the film *after* the ring was lost, but in actuality was shot *before* the shower scene. (Remember, films are not shot in sequence.)

We had a huge cast of well-known actors in this film, and I would like you to know that all of them were very pleasant to work with. Each actor has his or her own unique temperament (they're people, just like you and me), so it's important to observe each one closely and get to know when is and when isn't a good time to approach them about a particular prop. Some actors start getting into character as they leave their trailers and head to set, and are very often mentally preparing and/or going over their lines in their head. This is an example of when not to interrupt them. Some seem to stay in character all day long, while others can be hanging out on stage waiting for their scene while talking, laughing, or even joking around, and don't get into character until the cameras are about to roll. My M.O. is to give them their space and try to pick the right time to have a brief discussion only when necessary. That has always worked well for me.

Other questions that come up in conversation about *Apollo 13* involve the lunar module. One has to do with what appears to be weightlessness, and the other is about the times in the script when the systems are powered down, causing the extremely cold temperature in the spacecraft, resulting in the audience being able to see the actors' breath.

When the scene contained dialogue and the actor(s) needed to appear weightless, they were sitting on one end of a specially rigged teeter-totter that was being controlled on the other end by a special effects person. That is what gave the illusion of weightlessness, and also why if you watch the film and look at the shots, you'll notice that the audience never sees below a certain point. However, there are brief periods in the film where you do see their full bodies accompanied by objects floating in the air. In those scenes, they really were weightless, as were the cameraman, Ron, and a few key crew members. They were able to achieve this by building the lunar module set inside a plane known as the "KC 135 Vomit Comet". The Vomit Comet is a plane used to simulate weightlessness for astronauts. It's a hollowed-out Boeing 707 with padded walls that allow its passengers to be gravity-free by taking a steep dive from 30,000 feet in the air. I was not part of this crew, but I heard the guys that were, really enjoyed the experience... once they were able to control their nausea.

As far as creating the extreme cold in the spacecraft during the crisis, there was no illusion involved. There was only one way to achieve this. Huge air conditioners were brought onto the stage to get the temperature cold enough to see one's breath. Misters were also installed to raise the humidity levels. The misters were installed overhead and when they were needed, the assistant director would yell out, "Misters on!" and when they weren't, the command was, "Misters off!" These quickly were given the nicknames 'Mr. Zahn' and 'Mr. Zoff.'

My daughter, Danielle, who was only thirteen at the time, but had heard me talking about the conditions on the set, came to me with a note she had written to Ron asking him if her dad could be excused from having to work on the stage while it was being refrigerated. She didn't want her daddy to have to be cold. It was such a cute little note. (See inserted photograph.) Danielle is now thirty-one years old, is the proud mother of my little granddaughter, Riley Grace, and has another baby daughter on the way.

Should any of you see the film for the first, second, or even the third time, you now have an idea and a new perspective regarding what it takes to make a major motion picture. With this new found knowledge, my hope is that you'll take the time to not only check out the props, but also gain more of an appreciation as you watch scene by scene, the extensive research, hard work, talent and creativity that goes into a project like *Apollo 13*.

CHAPTER 20

2 Days in the Valley

Just as I was finishing *Apollo 13*, I received a call to interview with John Herzfeld, the writer/director of the film, *2 Days in the Valley*. John is very intense but he is not unreasonable. He had very specific ideas about his film. I appreciate that because it is far better to work with a director who knows what he wants. The job becomes far more difficult with a director that waffles back and forth and has a hard time making up his/her mind.

This was only a two-man crew for my department. Jimmy "Bean Skins" Robinson would once again be my assistant. It was imperative to be as well prepared as possible, because having to leave the location for any reason would have left only one man on set, increasing the potential for problems.

Our production designer was Catherine Hardwicke, who has gone on to be a very successful director. She directed the well received film *Thirteen* and directed the first of the *Twilight* series. Every day, she wore a paper-mache bird in her hair on top of her head, resembling a small finch. It was the kind you can buy in an arts-and-crafts store.

One day early on in the shooting while Jimmy and I were busy on set, Catherine came up and asked me to show her all of the props for the film that I had on our truck. This kind of thing always astonishes me because it makes no sense to leave the set shorthanded in the middle of shooting for a request like that. Plus, remember that I told you before that the prop truck is always parked the farthest from set and in this case it was a short drive away. Anyway, I refused to do it right then, but offered to give her a tour of the truck at a later time. I remember her being less than thrilled by my response, but that was how it had to be. As head of the department, I am responsible for assessing priorities at any given moment so that they serve the project's best interests as well as my own.

* * *

John had assembled a very impressive ensemble cast. Interestingly, he cast Charlize Theron in a sizable role. At that time, Charlize was just twenty years old and had almost no acting experience. Prior to this film, she had been a model from South Africa. I have no idea how John came to cast her in the film, but she was very good in spite of her lack of experience. There is one scene in particular where she really had an opportunity to shine, and she certainly did. It is the scene with James Spader seducing her in a motel room. James is an exceptional talent and a very intense actor. This being her first film, and a nude scene at that, she amazingly held her own. Personally, I think it turned out to be one of the film's finest moments. You've got to hand it to John for seeing something special in her and giving her this break.

In addition to her being absolutely gorgeous, she was one of the sweetest women with whom I have worked. Charlize, as we have all seen, has gone on to have a very successful career winning an Oscar for Best Actress for her portrayal of Eileen Warnos (the serial killer who has since been executed), in the film, *Monster*. Charlize was magnificent in that role and I was very excited to see her receive that prestigious award.

I worked with her again the year after *2 Days in the Valley* on a film entitled, *Trial and Error*. This was her fourth film. One day while shooting a difficult scene, Charlize needed some extra help from our director Jonathan Lynn. For some reason it was taking longer than anyone expected, when I heard a snide comment from a crew member, "Someone give Charlize a paper bag and see if she can act her way out." I wonder what that jerk thought as she walked up to the podium that Oscar night to accept her Best Actress award.

* * *

Eric Stoltz had the role of an undercover cop working the beat with Jeff Daniels, who portrayed an angry cop hell-bent on busting a newly opened Asian massage parlor. One particular scene had Eric getting a massage, but only for the purpose of trying to obtain incriminating evidence against the establishment. He finds himself enjoying the massage given by a beautiful young Asian girl. At one point, Eric, naked, other than a towel draped over his private parts, is supposed to get aroused as some of the dialogue revolves around his having an erection. Well... it was the prop department to the rescue (as I had anticipated would be the case), supplying a dildo to achieve what the scene called for. I don't know about you other men, but acting on camera in front of a room full of people and being able to achieve a hard on and keep it up between cuts and changing camera angles seemed like a pretty lofty goal to me. If you see the scene, you will notice that my dildo, which was fondly given the name, "Mr. Happy," did an admirable job as a stand-in boner!

* * *

There is another interesting scene toward the end of the film that involved a huge shoot out that took place at a location in Malibu canyon. Malibu is a very wealthy, exclusive beach community about twenty-five miles north of Santa Monica. I was instructed to have full loads for all of the weapons. Full loads are the most powerful and loudest of the blank ammunition we have available to us. For gun enthusiasts who are wondering how a semi-automatic weapon can fire repeatedly without an actual projectile, this is how it is accomplished. All of our guns are plugged with a custom-fitted piece in the end of the barrel that allows enough pressure to build up when fired with blank ammo to chamber the next round. As a result, we have to be very careful to load the proper-sized blank into the corresponding weapon. If we were to load a full load blank into a pistol rigged to fire quarter loads, the weapon would blow up in our hands when discharged.

Should there be a scene in which the camera can see down the barrel, we would have to remove that piece. Otherwise, it stays in the weapon throughout the shoot. That first night in Malibu I must have gone through at least 200 rounds of ammo. Add that amount of firepower to the noise generated by the full loads, and you have a recipe for some serious complaints.

Every location we use requires a permit and needs to stipulate what the surrounding residents should expect. Apparently, the neighbors weren't informed that this night of shooting was going to sound like the beginning of World War III. The complaints reached the local mayor's office; and early the next day, I got a call from an agitated location manager (the person in charge of locations and shooting permits). He had been notified that no more loud gunfire was allowed. *Great! We hadn't finished the previous night's sequence and needed more gunfire tonight*! This put me in a hell of a spot. I was now on the hook to either have the guns re-plugged to shoot quarter-loads, which would be substantially less offensive, or get what are known as "non-guns" (replica weapons that shoot electronic charges but make very little noise).

The issue was problematic for a couple of reasons. All of this needed to be decided upon and remedied before returning to work that night. Non-guns are great for a certain type of shot; however, they show no action, meaning that for the semi-auto weapons the chamber does not open and close upon firing and you don't see casings being ejected. For revolvers, the hammer stays fixed and the barrel does not rotate.

I had little choice but to do whatever was necessary to make it work. It took me the entire day to get it done. Having an armorer re-plug some of the weapons to use quarter loads, and to use non-guns for the rest, solved the problem. *Looks like I picked the wrong day to get some sleep!*

Just a short note: There is a scene in the film where a car is stolen from the curb directly in front of a gay bar. The license plate reads, "Ride Me". That was my idea. I thought it was a nice little touch.

Less than two years later I received a call from a producer of an HBO movie that John was going to direct about Don King, the famous fight promoter with the electric hair. I was available and happy to be doing another project with him.

CHAPTER 21

I Still Know What You Did Last Summer

During the early part of 1998, the producer who had hired me for *The Cable Guy* offered me the job on *I Still Know What You Did Last Summer*, the sequel to *I Know What You Did Last Summer*.

We shot on the Sony lot, local locations around Los Angeles, and then traveled to Mexico for the final three weeks of filming. We were somewhere between Puerto Vallarta and Manzanillo and stayed in a nice vacation resort. The star, Jennifer Love Hewitt (a very sweet young lady) was nineteen years old at the time. Our director was a young English fellow who stood about 5'2" tall. I couldn't really tell during the preparation period what the little chap would be like on set, but it became evident early on.

One night we shot a scene with the *bad fisherman* lying presumably dead in the middle of the street. As you know the protocol by now, I had gotten approval in advance from the director for a dummy that I thought would work well as the dead body. When I brought the dummy on set, suddenly he didn't like it anymore. Sound familiar?

He starting yelling at me and made a nasty comment about this not being an amateur film. He told me to find a way to make the head swivel.

Luckily, our special effects coordinator did just that. It was exactly as the director had requested, but once again he rejected the entire thing saying the dummy did not resemble a dead body. He then ordered the stand-in (a person who resembles an actor in height, weight, and coloring) to get into the fisherman's wardrobe so he could be the dead body. The director got behind the camera and told the poor guy where to place himself in the street. One would assume that the stand-in now sprawled out on the pavement on his stomach, lying perfectly still, would do the trick. NOPE!!!! Our little director started yelling again that even this idea sucked and the stand-in didn't look like a dead body either. At this point, I wasn't sure what the guy wanted, but I had no plans to actually murder somebody, throw the fisherman's clothes on him, and dump him in the middle of the street! He finally calmed down and settled for the stand-in.

Nothing else really stands out in my mind until we got to Mexico, where it was the middle of summer and very hot and sticky. For some reason, every afternoon the director would yell at the crew and tell us to hurry up with whatever it was we were doing at the time. He would rant and rave for a bit and then go sit down. At least he wasn't pointing the finger at one person; just letting us know in general that he felt we should be moving faster.

There was one particular young actor he didn't like. We had a scene in which this unfortunate kid had to be hit across the head with a boat paddle. Naturally, I had several paddles that were made of soft rubber. The director had the actor who was swinging the paddle hit this kid so many times that I was running out of paddles. These rubber doubles are not designed to clobber a person over and over again. Normally a director wouldn't allow his actor to be hit that many times. None of us ever knew whether the director was really that unsatisfied with how the scene was going or if he just enjoyed seeing this kid get smacked repeatedly.

* * *

Our production office, the actors, and the "above the line" people were staying in the upper bungalows of the resort, and the rest of the crew stayed down the hill in the lower bungalows. I had information that needed to be faxed to Los Angeles. In order to get up to the production office, I had to climb about ninety brick stairs that were built into the steep hill.

I started up the stairs and at about the fourth or fifth stair I heard something. A large coconut had fallen from one of the palm trees and began bouncing down the hill right towards me. This was not the little brown coconut most of us are used to seeing, but a coconut still in the large green husk. I froze in my tracks thinking it would hit a rock or something and veer off course, which it didn't do. It all happened very quickly, but I remember flashing on that huge boulder coming down the hill in *Raiders of the Lost Ark*.

By this point, it had picked up plenty of speed and it was clear that if I didn't do something fast, this fuckin' thing was going to hit me. At the last second, I literally dove into the side of that hill, the coconut barely missing my head. If it had hit me at that speed it would have been "lights out"! In a slight state of shock, I noticed that the nail from my big toe had been almost completely torn off, due to wearing only flip-flops at the time. Relieved to still be alive, I continued my trek up the stairway to take care of business.

When I got to the offices, someone immediately phoned the doctor who was on call at the resort. He comes up with his doctor's bag to take a look. His English was not good, but he wanted to know how this had happened. When I finally was able to convey to him what had taken place, he began to laugh. In broken English, he told us that he had been walking up and down that hill for eight years without ever once having such an incident. What could I say? *I'm just lucky, I guess.* The funny thing is a lot of the crew really didn't believe that I was telling the truth. I took a lot of ribbing about it and one night a stunt guy snuck up behind me and rolled a coconut right by where I was standing. Naturally, it startled me, and everyone had a good laugh at my expense.

So, I'm sitting there with the doctor as he examines the nail still barely hanging on to my toe. "I'm going to have to take the whole knee off," he says.

"KNEE???" I shrieked, "There is nothing wrong with my knee!!" As I said, his English was poor and what he meant to say was the whole *nail*, not the *knee*. What a relief!

I sent off my fax, and following the doctor, limped toward his office. He really did a good job preventing infection and taking good care of me in general. It was painful as hell and it did keep me off the set for a couple of days. It took an entire year for my nail to heal and grow back. I still get razzed whenever I run into someone who worked with me on that show.

Another incident that took place was our experience shooting in a mango grove. This location had been scouted during pre-production; and no one realized that by the time we would actually be shooting this sequence, the location would be completely infested with the most disgusting beetles known to man. We were on a graveyard set and these beetles were crawling all over the walls, the gravestones, everywhere. There were so many of them, the camera was picking them in the shots. Something needed to be done. The effects guys sprayed them with some sort of heavy-duty chemical, but it didn't faze them.

To make matters worse, they were also up in the trees, and this scene was being shot "in the rain" which of course was rigged by our effects team. When the rainwater was turned on, hundreds of beetles were washed out of the trees and down onto us!! *Agghhhh!!* We all had to seal ourselves up as well as possible to keep them from falling down our shirts. I got a big hat and some netting to put over me, and I also tied off the bottom of my pants to keep them from crawling up my legs.

As if it couldn't get any worse, these bastards would either bite or sting—or whatever it is they do—and when they did, it hurt like hell and emitted the worst odor you have ever smelled. The sting would also leave a huge mark on the skin that looked like a burn. The actors obviously couldn't wear hats or protective covering so we would hold umbrellas over their heads when they were off camera. If I remember correctly, Jennifer was a sting victim.

It was a horrendous night and I have never been so happy to hear the word, "Wrap."

CHAPTER 22

Transition into Television

In 1998, at the completion of *I Still Know What You Did Last Summer*, I took a long motorcycle trip from Los Angeles to New York, planning on hanging out in the Big Apple for a week or two. It turned out to be a solo journey, as the two other guys that were going to ride with me took shows they could not afford to turn down.

Riding a motorcycle across the country had always been something I'd dreamt about. I suppose the idea first entered my mind after seeing *Easy Rider* in 1969. Riding motorcycles is something I love and have been doing since I was 16 years old. In 1994, I purchased my first brand-new Harley Davidson (which I still own and ride today) and by 1998, felt comfortable enough to take the journey alone. I decided to make it a one-way trip and have the bike shipped back to Los Angeles. This allowed me more time to enjoy the sights along the way without the worry of having to ride all the way back home.

Thank God, I had a safe journey with only one really scary experience. Being from California I had not been familiar with the weather patterns across the states. All went fine until I found myself between Cody and Buffalo, Wyoming. It was late in the afternoon and the sun was shining. However I noticed the sky suddenly darkening and I began to see lightening in the distance. As I continued east I soon became alarmed, as what had been distant flashes were now bolts of lightening that were much closer to where I was, and there was absolutely no place to seek cover. These bolts had an ominous look to them. In the past I had seen flashes of light or smaller bolts, but these were nasty, jagged, frightening bolts the likes of which I had never seen. I put my head down, and in the pouring rain, continued until I arrived in Buffalo. A hot shower, dinner, and a full night's sleep were all I needed to be ready for the next day's ride.

About a week later, as I was crossing the Verrazano Bridge and saw the New York skyline in the distance, I realized I had accomplished a childhood dream. As I guided my motorcycle toward Brooklyn Harley Davidson, where I was to drop the bike off, I had an interesting moment. Stopped at a red light in front of a pizza joint, I saw a group of Italian guys sitting outside laughing and talking about bustin' each other's balls. Just like *Goodfellas*! Then it hit me; *I actually rode a motorcycle from coast to coast!*

I had been in New York for about a week and was enjoying myself when out of the blue I received a call from Los Angeles. I was asked to immediately fly home to start a high-profile large-budget film. This was not in my plans, but I thought about the money I would make and chose to do what was asked of me. I flew home and started work. The transition from a month-long trip, to an office on the Sony Studio lot with a script in my hand, proved difficult for me to adjust to. Sunday I was partying in the Big Apple; Monday, I'm unexpectedly flying home; and Tuesday I'm at work.

The end result was that from approximately September '98 until March '99, I entered the darkest period of my life. I fell into a depression. I was just unable to function. I could see no alternative other than quitting my job. As time passed and I remained in a depressed state, I reached out for help. After about six weeks, I started feeling a bit more like my old self again. Slowly but surely I began to make baby steps toward recovery. I knew I had to get back to work but was not ready to take on a stressful project. All property master positions are stressful, so I came up with the idea of returning but as an assistant instead of being the department head.

It was 1999 and I hadn't been an assistant since 1978. I was smart enough not to let pride stand in the way of my health, so it was not a difficult choice to make. I began researching for ways to become an assistant, when I happened to come across the property master of a TV show some of you might remember entitled *V.I.P.*, starring Pamela Anderson.

It was also during this time that I met and married my current wife Deanna. We met shortly after I was hired on *V.I.P.* The timing was perfect because I was making real progress coming out of that six-month depression. Meeting Deanna was a critical factor for me in terms of speeding up my recovery. We met in April and were married in November of 1999. As of this writing, we have been together for over 14 years and my life has continuously gotten better.

While working on this show I was shopping for some off-the-wall prop, when I came across a very funny remote-controlled fart machine. Quite unlike the type that Leslie Nielson had on *Airplane*, this was a modernized version. One part was a small remote control unit very close in size to that of a garage door opener that could fit on your key ring. The other part was shaped like an old-fashioned jukebox, but was black and fit into the palm of your hand. This was the part that would emit the fart sound when the remote button was activated. This machine had five distinctly different sounding farts, all very real. Of course I had to purchase one, as I knew I would get some laughs with it.

When I returned to the stage that day, the mood was unusually light, so I decided to give my new acquisition a trial run. I went over to talk with our script supervisor and very carefully dropped the fart box into the pocket that hung from the side of his director's chair. I walked a good fifteen feet away, and when the stage went quiet for a rehearsal, I hit the remote, cranking out a nasty sounding fart. Everyone cracked up, except the poor script supervisor, whom everyone was now pointing fingers at. As he was trying to declare his innocence, (which no one was buying), I let loose with another, resulting in more hysterics. Now I felt it time to reveal the true source of the farts and avoid further embarrassment to the poor guy. I casually walked over and pulled the farter from his script pocket. No one had ever seen such an advanced unit, and our lead actress, Pam, asked me where I bought it. She then asked me to purchase fifteen units for her. I obliged and ordered them. The total came to $350.00 that I put on my credit card. Of course she said she would reimburse me.

When I received the farters I told her bodyguard that they had arrived and asked him to let her know. He said he needed for me to give him five farters immediately, as Pam wanted to add them to gift baskets she was giving away. I handed them over and asked him to get me a check or cash for the total amount, handing him a copy of the receipt. One week passed, and I again requested the money. Two, three, four more weeks passed and still nothing. I didn't approach Pam myself because he assured me that she was fully aware that she owed me the money and I would get it. I never did. I ate the cost of the five units that I initially gave him, but I kept the rest. I really didn't need ten fart machines, but over the course of a few years I gave them away to people who really appreciated them. Well worth it in the end!

CHAPTER 23

True Blood

First of all–let me congratulate Stephen Moyer not only for landing a leading roll in a hit television series, but for marrying the smokin' hot Anna Paquin who has publicly announced that she is bisexual. Talk about every man's dream!

Season One was really great. Like most episodic television, we had long hours and difficult days, but we had an excellent line producer and unit production manager. They put together a great crew that they really cared about, and they were right there in the trenches with us throughout the season. They listened to the department heads when difficulties arose and worked with us to resolve them. The season turned out to be a bigger hit than anticipated by HBO, rivaling the numbers (amount of viewers) that *The Sopranos* had for its first season. We indeed had the kind of leadership that made us happy to go that extra mile. When the hours and amount of work became a strain for my two on-set prop people (Bryan and Bill), we were granted another set person in order to continue the quality of work we were providing.

The cast, all very talented young actors, were mostly easy to work with. When working with talented and creative people, it's inevitable that new ideas will be bantered about and can result in last-minute changes. It is our job to assist in any way we can to accommodate those changes, but in many cases the new ideas can be challenging. Most props are discussed and pre-approved by the director, either in meetings or what we call a "show and tell". A show and tell is a display of the key props for the director and producers to look over and approve prior to a new episode being shot.

In terms of last-minute requests, with the actors playing the roles of *Jason* (*Sookie's* brother) and *Lafayette* (the flamboyant gay chef), they had a tendency to come up with last-minute ideas for unscripted props, either at on-set rehearsals or just prior to cameras rolling.

One example: This particular scene had *Jason* entering *Gran's* house before heading upstairs to his room. During the rehearsal he asked if he could go to the refrigerator first, and grab a leftover sausage. The problem was that we had not yet shot the scene where the sausages are introduced, so we didn't have any cooked sausages standing by. This left us with about twelve minutes to come up with the sausages. Now our focus had to be on scrambling to manifest this prop request. Fortunately, the studio's commissary was open and had sausages, so they were able to whip several up for me on the spot. We got lucky, but what if the commissary wasn't open? What if they didn't have any sausages? Spur-of-the-moment ideas create a lot of stress and anxiety for our department.

Here are a couple of examples of what could have been harder and more problematic last-minute requests: *Lafayette* is in his house, paranoid of an attack by someone he has wronged. The scene calls for his cousin *Tara* to knock on his front door. I was on the prop truck and got a call on my two-way radio. During rehearsal he decided he wanted a large kitchen knife and a bat. My initial thought was, *uh oh, this sounds dangerous!* The first thing I needed to find out was exactly how these were going to be used. I went to the set to discuss this with the director. If anyone should get hurt at anytime with a prop, it's automatically my fault. Had these items been pre-approved or discussed, I would have had soft rubber versions made if necessary. I did have a real bat and a large kitchen knife on the prop truck, but I sure wasn't going to allow them to be used in an unsafe manner. It turned out *Lafayette* simply wanted to grab a knife and pick up the bat, and when he saw that it was *Tara* at the door, would set them both down.

That same day, we had another close call involving *Lafayette*. He was lying on his couch, supposedly recovering from a gunshot wound. It had been discussed that he would have some prescription pill bottles, a glass of water, and a bottle of vodka on the coffee table. Drugs and alcohol are never to be consumed on camera simultaneously unless a phony label is placed on the liquor bottle. (These are known as non-descript, or n.d. labels). No liquor company wants their product associated with drunkenness or drug abuse, but they are willing to give us free product as long as it is used appropriately. The vodka on the table in this scene was a name brand being promoted by a friend of an executive at HBO.

I was not on set but was informed by an assistant that *Lafayette* decided to take the pills and wash them down with the vodka (not a scripted action). The pills were placebo and the vodka bottle contained water, but that was not the point. The point was that a mistake was made allowing a real brand of liquor to be mixed with the consumption of pills. When my assistant on set told me about this, I was very upset. The next morning I called the post-production supervisor and explained my dilemma. They were able to cut to a shot of *Tara*, thus eliminating a possible costly error. Still, this was a mistake on our part and I was upset that it happened.

Now, a story of true dedication: One of the *True Blood* episodes called for a possum's penis to be worn around a character's neck. Apparently this is considered a good luck charm in some parts of the country. The thing basically resembles a curved thin bone. When I read it, I was thinking, *how in the hell am I going to come up with this?* I figured that I would research what it looks like and have it fabricated. Over that weekend, I called my assistant Bill's house to discuss this very issue. His wife told me he wasn't home, but that while he was out doing errands he saw a dead possum on the side of the road and had hidden it somewhere. He was now on his way with a cooler full of ice to retrieve it and take it to a taxidermist friend to find out if it was in fact a male. At first I thought she was kidding, but she WASN'T! *And* it did turn out to be male. That is how it came to be that we actually got our prop. No one I know other than Bill would go to that length for his job.

Another thing people would ask about. "What do you use for the drinkable blood; it looks so real?" At first we came up with a recipe that included mixing juices with different types of berries that we put into a blender. The problem was the berries had to be strained over and over to get the seeds out, but when finished, looked pretty good. We would make it darker and slightly brown for blood that had been spilled for a while, and thinner and redder for fresher blood. In the end, however, we were using purple carrot juice, which actually worked very well. For blood that is not to be consumed, we used several varieties specifically made for the film industry that look terrific but are not safe for human consumption.

Season Two also had a prop that I was frequently asked about. It was the mysterious soufflé that *Maryanne* had created and cooked for *Eggs* and *Tara* to eat. Unbeknownst to the characters, the soufflé, as delicious as it tasted, was supposedly made from the heart of *Daphne,* the shape shifter, who had been having a relationship with *Sam. Maryanne,* having put *Eggs* under her spell, had him kill *Daphne* and remove her heart while having no recollection of doing so. She then makes an extremely bloody yet tantalizing soufflé with *Daphne's* heart and entices *Tara* and *Eggs* to eat it. Consuming this pie sends them into a bizarre frenzy, keeping them further under *Maryanne's* control.

Accomplishing the look of this pie took some creative thinking. We incorporated the skills of the special-effects department and my food stylist Wendy, who was responsible for most of the on-camera food. First, we had to find something that both actors would agree to eat and would pass for chunks of a human heart. That turned out to be cooked chunks of chicken. Next was to create a very bloody sauce that was not only ominous looking but palatable enough to be eaten. Wendy spent time experimenting with different options until she arrived at a recipe that worked well for these requirements.

She also had to create a delicious-looking crust to make the dish appear to be a real soufflé. Once we had the working recipe, Wendy made several crusts and a gallon or two of the bloody "chunky heart sauce" filling that we gave to the special effects department to experiment with. The goal was to get a good shot of the blood oozing out of the pie as it was being cut into with a knife.

The effects guys cut a hole into the bottom of the table that the soufflé was sitting on, and another hole into the dish the soufflé was in. They then loaded a pump with the blood sauce. A tube was connected from the offstage pump, under the table and through the holes in the table and soufflé dish. The result being that, on action, the actor would cut into the soufflé with a large knife. At that moment the effects man watching from just offstage activated the blood-filled pump, causing the bloody substance to slowly ooze out of the cut, producing the extremely gruesome desired look. If you saw this episode, I'm sure you would agree it was quite effective.

* * *

Season Two unfortunately brought us two new leaders. For all of their hard work, efforts, and dedication creating a very successful first season, our line producer and unit production manager were released by HBO, having been told the series ran over budget. My team and I were very upset about this, as were many other crew members. Season One ran like a well-oiled machine, from our perspective. We were not happy to lose our team leaders and were skeptical of who might replace them.

We received a new executive producer (let's call him Gregg) and one new line producer/unit production manager. These guys were brought in first and foremost to keep expenses down, but in doing so made it a very unpleasant season. For example, they would have what is referred to as a splinter unit running frequently, which amounts to two separate crews working simultaneously. This not only made the job more difficult, but they were not accommodating in allowing us the amount of help needed to supply two units adequately. Of course they immediately added another production supervisor to their staff to help ease *their* load.

I saved Gregg embarrassment by bailing him out of a money-saving idea he had. Our actress, Michelle Forbes, who played the very dangerous *Maryanne* in Season Two, is in real life an animal proponent and very active in animal rights. She is also a vegetarian. One particular scene in an episode had her entering her house holding a freshly killed rabbit still dripping blood. Upon reading this, I contacted a company that makes replica animals. They happen to be endorsed by PETA (People for the Ethical Treatment of Animals.) I got an approximate price that I revealed at our concept meeting. After learning the price, Gregg instructed me to not order the rabbit due to the expense. He was going to have our special effects make-up department fabricate one using an actual rabbit pelt for a substantially lesser cost. I warned him that Michelle may not like that idea, and he had better check with her first. He told me not to worry about it. *Okay....*

A couple of days went by, and I got a 911 call from Gregg. He informed me that Michelle absolutely would not touch the rabbit pelt. Could I put a rush on the one I had suggested? Yes, I could, at twice the price originally quoted due to a rush charge.

As Season Two was coming to a conclusion, an issue arose that prompted a discussion I needed to have with Gregg. One of the production supervisors would not approve the amount of help I needed for a very busy night of work. I decided to go over her head and address this problem with Gregg, who remedied the situation immediately in my favor. We had a discussion about trust and how important it is to listen to the reasoning of the department heads. Shortly after this conversation, I received an email from Gregg expressing his approval of my work during that difficult season, and inviting me back for Season Three.

However, unbeknownst to him, I was not happy with my two Season Two on-set assistants. Bill had moved on to another project, and I needed Bryan to assist me in preparation due to the increased workload. The cast and everyone else on the crew really liked them, but they gave Bryan and me problems that no one else was aware of (we wanted to keep the inner department turmoil to ourselves), and they were not following directions that I was giving to them. It seemed that they were trying to constantly throw Bryan and me under the bus. At season's end, I fired them both. Gregg, however, was not pleased about that as he said the cast liked them very much. I assured him (through his right-hand man Mark) that I would find two other assistants that the cast would like equally as well. I made it clear that when I returned, I would not be bringing them back.

Well, something that is almost unheard of happened, and I did not return for Season Three. Let me explain. There are producers, such as those who we had for Season One, who trust and listen to their department heads. This results in a smoother running production. No one knows more about a department's needs than the head of that department. A good producer knows that. Gregg's ego in tandem with a poor decision to let me go ended up causing more problems. The irony of this whole situation is that he wound up doing exactly what I told him needed to be done in the first place!

What had transpired was, Gregg chose the two set assistants over Bryan and me. Another prop master was hired in my place and was instructed to keep the two assistants that I had the problems with. The new prop master was fired before Episode 3 was completed. He went to Gregg on his way out the door and explained his feelings of dismay concerning the two set people who were forced upon him. Still, he was relieved of duty. Another prop master was then brought in and was also instructed to keep the same two troublesome assistants. Three weeks later that prop master informed Gregg that he was quitting the show unless he could bring in his own people. He refused to continue to be held hostage by those two toxic set assistants he had been forced to use.

I guess the third time's a charm because Gregg finally got the message and fired the backstabbing duo. News travels fast in this industry, and it is no secret who the two people are. Let's just say that their opportunities for work have dwindled since then!

CHAPTER 24

Cut–Print–Wrap: Outtakes

I still have a handful of stories to share but none of them seemed to warrant an entire chapter. So here are some random thoughts and experiences to toss into the mix; my outtake files.

Years ago in the early 1980's I did a series called *The Renegades*. The show had an ensemble cast but the stand out was Patrick Swayze. This was long before he became a big star. Although I certainly can't claim to have known him well, I did spend time talking with him. Patrick was all about good. During the short course of that series we talked about several things, and if ever there was an honest, stand-up dude, it was Patrick. He was wise beyond his years, humble, and spoke about things like how much he loved his wife. This was a twenty-nine year old young man who could have had his head in the clouds, but instead had his feet firmly planted on the ground. Although I never saw or spoke with him after the series ended, I can't imagine he ever changed from the guy I knew back then.

* * *

I had the good fortune to work on two feature films directed by Carl Reiner. Carl goes back to early 50's television and did bits with people such as Sid Caesar, Imogene Coca, and Mel Brooks, among many others. He was the creative force behind the very successful *Dick Van Dyke Show* back in the 60's, and he played *Rob Petrie's* boss, *Alan Brady* on that series as well.

The films I propped for him were *All of Me* starring Steve Martin and Lily Tomlin, and *Summer School* with Mark Harmon and Kirstie Alley. Carl was a lot of fun to work for. He is not a screamer and treats people well. He has a great sense of humor and a keen mind. The result is a pleasant working atmosphere where everyone's work is allowed to shine.

I enjoyed the actors on his shows as well. Steve Martin was pleasant, but not at all the outgoing character he normally portrays. Lily Tomlin was very precise about her props, particularly a doll. The doll was an idea that Lily came up with herself and had a clear vision of how she wanted it to be made. It was a good learning experience for me to work that closely with her. At a little party we had one day, she gave me a big kiss in appreciation for tending carefully to her requests.

*   *   *

Besides *Cocoon* and *Apollo 13*, the other Ron Howard film I did was *Gung Ho*, starring Michael Keaton and Mimi Rogers. The film centered on the Japanese takeover of an American car plant. There was nowhere in the United States that would allow us to film on their assembly line, so we wound up in a Fiat plant in Buenos Aires, Argentina. It was an interesting and educational experience to work in that country. The hours were long, and it was cold and uncomfortable in the plant, but hey, it was a Ron Howard film and we had a good time.

* * *

As prop people we find ourselves periodically purchasing some rather strange things:

- 8 matching pink frilly panties

- 18 bottles of dollar-a-bottle wine

- A dozen tubes of lubricant with assorted sizes and colored dildos

- 6 quarts of prune juice

I think you get the idea. One of the funniest reactions I've experienced was when I had to buy a huge quantity of douche at a drug store. I must have bought the place out. I was standing in line with stacks of every brand and scent overflowing in my basket. As I began to unload them onto the checkout conveyer belt, I noticed the guy standing behind me staring at what I was about to purchase. Feeling a bit uncomfortable, I reached over to the candy stand, picked out a chocolate bar, and tossed it in front of the douche mound. The guy tapped me on the shoulder and as I turned around he said, "That'll throw 'em off!"

Epilogue

Since my time on *True Blood*, I have done 2 full seasons of episodic television and 5 pilots. The pilot that I really hoped would get a green light and that I would be a part of was entitled *Village People*. It was a sit-com, commonly known as a multi-camera show that is shot in front of a live audience. The creator was a wonderful and talented woman by the name of Meg Deloatch. I spent a few seasons with Meg in the past and was very excited at the prospect of working with her and her great group of people again. We had Jenny Garth as our lead actress, and shooting the pilot was really fun. In addition, my wife Deanna is in a band named *Wildwood Highway,* and one of their songs was chosen to open the show. When the networks announced the fall line-up, *Village People* was not on it. I was so disappointed. Selfishly so because I knew I would have had a great time on the job, but also disappointed for Meg, who had worked so hard for her project to be a success.

In recent years I had begun to think more about retirement. Now, at 61, and with 39 years of service and over 73,000 hours under my belt as a prop man, I was starting to feel like what my hero Willie Mays must have felt like when the San Francisco Giants traded him to the New York Mets at the tail end of his amazing career. Baseball fans will know exactly what I mean. It's not so much that my skills were eroding. The truth is that I wasn't very popular anymore. Many of the people that used to hire me had retired. I was no longer willing to travel for long periods of time, and I really didn't feel I had the energy to do the high-budget feature films that are popular today. Work was getting harder for me to come by, and my desire to do it was dissipating as well.

Looking back at the time I was a young and enthusiastic prop master, I remember talking to my peers about some of the older dudes I would talk to that had been propping films for many years. I remember telling my cohorts that these "old farts" sounded jaded and sour and were always reminiscing about the "good old days"—always complaining that things were no longer how they used to be and how much better they had once been.

You know, there is only one thing that stays the same, and that is change. Nothing is as it used to be, particularly in the work world. Changes are constantly going on at all levels. I have personally seen the industry change drastically during my long tenure. There are now local crews all over the country willing and able to do the jobs we used to be brought on location to do. Many states are giving the producers large tax incentives, further lessening the work pool from Hollywood. Currently there is more production going on in Georgia and Louisiana than there is in Hollywood. Budgets for below-the-liners have steadily decreased, as more money is poured into special visual effects and above-the-line costs. Below-the-line employees find themselves more often than not at odds with production managers, having to fight to get a fair price for their equipment rentals, salaries, and work force.

The issue in recent years I have had to come to terms with is that now it is me that sounds like the old guys I used to mock and laugh about. I'm the one complaining about current conditions and how much worse things are now than when I started. All things being equal, I'm sure those old guys thought they saw the same demise in their day that I think I have seen in mine. It will go on that way with the guys just starting out now that will retire in 35 or 40 years. I don't want to go out as a cranky old guy, complaining about the state of the industry.

I made a choice. I retired last month. The only job I have ever known has come to an end. There is more to life than one's occupation. My time to begin to experience those things is now. As the years have passed, I have become far more spiritually inclined. None of us know what tomorrow will bring. I am so grateful for the health I enjoy and the health of my loved ones. I do not take that gift for granted. There are many things I hope to continue to be able to do, and many things I would like to be able to do for my wife, my kids, and my grandkids.

My years in this industry have been difficult. It is truly a stressful line of work. It's a lot less glamorous than it seems to outsiders if you are a below-the-line employee. However, I am very grateful that it provided me a way to support my family and myself. Were there drawbacks, particularly when it came to family life? Sure there were. But, I got to do things and see places, and work with people that most folks only dream about. It sure beat working in a cubicle or putting in eight hours a day in a retail store.

I certainly hope that I have accomplished the goal I had in mind when I decided to write this book, which was to provide the movie-going public a glimpse of what life is really like for a Hollywood crew member. I wanted them to see films from a new and different perspective. Not to be distracted from the plot, but to have a discussion after the film about what it took to provide them with what they had just witnessed on the screen. I realize, of course, that I am coming from a property master's point of view. Our job is so critical to the look of a film, yet we are not recognized by the Academy. I want this book to bring honor and recognition to my hard-working brothers and sisters of the prop depart-

ment. I want people to know that our job is as equally important as any of the more recognized departments.

I also wanted to illustrate the lighter side of the job by
bringing up the funny stories and interesting situations we
commonly find ourselves in. I wanted to educate, illuminate,
and bring smiles to my readers. After all, isn't that what
entertainment is all about?

About the Author

During his 39-year career, Levine logged more than 73,000 hours working in the film industry. He worked with many well-known directors and actors—and an assortment of personalities and egos. Since 1973, when he took his first film crew job, Levine has served as property master or assistant property master on more than thirty feature films and countless episodes of television productions, many of which are featured in *HOLLYWOOD From Below the Line*.

Levine grew up in a Hollywood family. His father, Allan Levine, was a longtime property master and founded the well-known prop rental house, *The Hand Prop Room*, still in operation on Venice Boulevard in Los Angeles.

Steven currently lives with his wife and two dogs in Manhattan Beach, California.

Film Credits

The Last Tycoon, 1976
10, 1978
Airplane, 1979
Hard Country, 1980
All of Me, 1983
Cocoon, 1984
Pee-wee's Big Adventure, 1985
Gung Ho, 1985
Smooth Criminal (music video), 1987
Jumpin' Jack Flash, 1987
Summer School, 1987
Cocoon:The Return, 1988
Havana, 1990
Rush, 1991
Born Yesterday, 1992
When a Man Loves a Woman, 1993
Higher Learning, 1994
Apollo 13, 1995
2 Days in the Valley, 1996
Cable Guy, 1997
Trial and Error, 1997
Why Do Fools Fall in Love, 1998
I Still Know What You Did Last Summer, 1998

Television Credits

The Renegades, 1980
More Wild Wild West, 1980
Cop Rock, 1990
For the People, 2002
American Family, 2002–2004
True Blood, 2008–2009
Glory Daze, 2010–2011
House of Lies, 2012